ACTING WITH
PASSION

ACTING WITH PASSION

A Performer's Guide to Emotions on Cue

NIKI FLACKS

Illustrations by Will Timbers
Photographs by Joel Horovitz

Bloomsbury Methuen Drama
An Imprint of Bloomsbury Publishing Plc

B L O O M S B U R Y
LONDON · NEW DELHI · NEW YORK · SYDNEY

Bloomsbury Methuen Drama

An imprint of Bloomsbury Publishing Plc

Imprint previously known as Methuen Drama

50 Bedford Square	1385 Broadway
London	New York
WC1B 3DP	NY 10018
UK	USA

www.bloomsbury.com

BLOOMSBURY, METHUEN DRAMA and the Diana logo are trademarks of Bloomsbury Publishing Plc

First published 2015
Reprinted by Bloomsbury Academic 2015

British Library Cataloguing-in-Publication Data
A catalogue record for this book is available from the British Library.

ISBN: PB: 978-1-4081-8373-1
ePDF: 978-1-4725-5731-5
ePUB: 978-1-4-081-8581-0

Library of Congress Cataloging-in-Publication Data
A catalog record for this book is available from the Library of Congress

Typeset by RefineCatch Limited, Bungay, Suffolk
Printed and bound in Great Britain

I would sink yet lower and be an actress or an opera singer, imperilling my soul by the wicked lie of pretending to be somebody else.

Misalliance, George Bernard Shaw

For all the actors who opened their hearts to explore this very different approach to acting – 'imperilling their souls' by tasting the joy of it 'being too easy'. Your courage, ambition, passion and dreams echo through every page of this book.

CONTENTS

PROLOGUE:
THE JOURNEY BEGINS

By age seventeen I wanted to be an actor more than anything in the world. I entered my drama school ready to learn my craft. The gold standard in training at the time was the Stanislavski Method. I spent hours 'visualizing', 'feeling cold and hot', and many more hours doing 'emotional recall'. I would remember when my cat Muffy died and I would weep. I also covered my scripts in notes. In the margins were my objectives and verbs to describe my actions: 'to provoke, to placate, to seduce'. I improvised my characters' past experiences, or the animals they might resemble and wrote detailed inner monologues. I did it all *with total commitment*. And then one day in Shakespeare class . . .

I was late to class and found myself literally running up the steps to the stage and into the scene. I didn't have time for *any of my vitally important preparation – rekindling sense memory and emotional recall*. Instead in a panic at being so late, magic happened. Juliet came alive. Excitement alternated with tears springing to my eyes and shy laughter moments later. After the scene our teacher, a frightening martinet, praised me to the skies. She told the class to notice how I *had played out my objectives* so clearly, how I had used *sense memory* to create the night and *emotional recall* to fall in love before our eyes.

I left class with my *terrible secret* – I had thought about *none* of those things and yet had been successful. In fact I had no idea what I'd done, other than the fact that it had been delicious. During my remaining years of study I became intrigued with these *disobedient lapses*.

My personal journey exploring, and then teaching the joys of 'disobedience'

My entry into that deepest spontaneity – which I was determined to figure out – was certainly not new. Artists, scientists, writers, actors, mathematicians – creative people have always searched for that 'holy grail'.

In *your quest* for this knowledge I invite you to join me, with all the twists and turns of my adventure. We will enter the extraordinary world of neuroscience and mind-body psychology. Again, and again, we will see that the answers lie in trusting the body. You will read about the ways you can cue your body with movement and sensory feedback to really experience *emotions on cue*.

To give you a taste and insight, I'm going to share with you some comments from actors I have trained all over the world.

ACTORS' TESTIMONIALS

Actors who have studied with me say . . .

I have worked with many teachers over the fifty years that I have been in the theatre. I studied with Bobby Lewis, also with the Atlantic Theater Company – W.H. Macy, Scott Zeigler and David Mamet. I was a member of the Open Theater, and La Mama Plexus who worked in their own method inspired by Grotowski. Niki Flacks is a trail-blazer and so it's not possible to say, 'Her work is like this or that.' The hardest thing for me to wrap my head around now, after fifty years of training, is that preparation could be so easy and effective. I'm finally 'in the moment' every moment.

Ken Glickfeld, New York

After traditional training at drama school in Paris and five years of Meisner training, Niki helped me become more familiar with all the different emotions which were bottled up inside of me, and showed me a way of feeling them in a non-destructive way to use them for acting on camera. Directors love that I can be so emotionally available every take.

Sophie Gilbert-Desvallons, Paris

I received years of intense training where I was bombarded with the Method and numerous tools to try and unearth psychological truth. However, Niki's work has provided me a stress free, failsafe way of working, a freedom no other way of working has ever supported.

Helen Millar, London

Niki's work is like nothing I've ever experienced before. I had trained in all sorts of physical techniques before including Lecoq, Alexander and Kabuki as well as Meisner and Method, but Niki's is different to any of these. You use your body as the instrument and the core purpose of *self-tuning* is to open up a 'channel' within you so that your full spectrum of emotions are free to bubble up to be accessed as and when you need them. The most moving and emotionally true work I've ever seen has not been at top-notch theatres, but in Niki's classes.

Chloe Welsh, Australia and London

I trained at the Arts Educational Drama School: the Method, improvization, Alexander technique and 'Framework'. Niki Flacks' class was so different than anything I had previously experienced. Nothing before gave me the sense of physical freedom and emotional openness. Immediately I began to audition more successfully.

Helen Stern, London and New York

I have taught Meisner for many years and was never comfortable with his Method-based 'Preparation'. It seemed contrary to his other techniques. When I experienced one of Niki's classes I knew immediately that her work is the perfect partnership for Meisner.

Scott Williams, San Francisco and London

Niki Flacks' work is the closest thing to real magic I have ever experienced. That the body's tissue contains memory is one step, to experience and relive that emotion is a giant leap.

Jack Price, Bristol

You can see that for those actors this work **either gave them a whole new approach or supported and made their techniques that much easier with an added dimension**. That has been my experience for all the years I've taught. Other *teachers of acting* have sometimes been curious, often outraged. Teachers of movement, already mind-body oriented, have generally been quite pleased to see how this approach reinforces their efforts.

My search begins

Let's go back to the beginning – I was leaving my Shakespeare class. My frustration was that I *didn't have a clue* as to how to make that magic happen again. Our movement and voice classes – considered our 'instrument work' – often led to a similar feeling of physical freedom, but I couldn't figure out how to move that into the 'acting' and remembering when my cat died.

Like so many actors, I was accustomed to hearing a constant stream of instructions, expectations, directions and criticisms coming from a voice in my head. I was certainly *concentrating and focusing* on all the things I believed would make the scene work. The lack of spontaneity, the struggle for making those emotions surge, I assumed was my limitation. But I somehow knew that if only I could get *rid of that voice as I did on my disobedient lapses*, I could do it all with ease.

The voice in the head is clearly the enemy. When I learned how to bypass the head and go directly into body I began calling my critical voice, *the Intellect*, as my revenge against the various teachers and directors who had shouted out, 'Stop intellectualizing!' when I was working so hard to visualize or remember something. What completely *unhelpful* advice. Instead, the Intellect just gets more abusive. 'You are hopeless! You're doing it again!' I'll be referring to *the Intellect* a great deal!

My hunger to find the way into spontaneity coincided with a parallel search in the fields of psychology, acting and neuroscience. The book, *The Primal Scream* was a bestseller. The Actors Studio bragged about the remarkable stars they had trained and spread their influence to drama schools everywhere. Most remarkable of all, a disciple of Freud's, Wilhelm Reich, came to believe that emotions were *locked in the muscles of the body and that through movement and with the release of muscular tension, emotions would pour forth.*

Reich's theories set me on fire. I realized that the moment-to-moment acting I wanted was coming from the unconscious mind. Somehow the unconscious (believed, at that time, to be dwelling only in the brain) was *connected* to the body. I explored. I experimented. The more I learned to access the unconscious *the more I began to feel it and visualize it in the centre of my body, like a dungeon where the emotions were an 'oppressed people',* guarded by the Intellect. **I began calling it my Dungeon.** So when I refer to the Intellect and the Dungeon – the two opposing forces we actors face constantly – you will know I'm talking about the Inner Critic and the unconscious mind.

In looking for therapists and acting teachers working with these concepts, I kept bumping up against the traditional belief in the use of memory to create feelings. This concept was deeply embedded in both worlds of acting and psychology. The acting teachers who chose to use the body to release feelings were trained at the Actors Studio. They taught *emotional recall* and *what if*, then adding movement, hoping the physical work would intensify the feelings.

Every time I would attempt to couple the emotional recall with the physical/emotional release, I was instantly back in my head trying to make the feelings bigger, or more interesting! Finally, I began to try *only the physical approach* with much better results. Again and again I would find entry into my Dungeon, moment to moment, emotions on cue.

Trusting this, quite naturally my career blossomed. At the age of twenty-three, I did my first Broadway play. I did film and television (the 'bad girl' on a soap for several years) and subsequently worked at most of the major regional repertory theatres in America – playing some of the best roles ever written with extraordinary directors and actors.

With this success I wanted to share what I learned. I resisted because I knew this approach was essentially psycho*therapy. I knew that was dangerous territory for an acting class.*

The current (the late 1960s and 70s) climate of Method training encouraged a great deal of not just remembering past abuse and sadness but then *talking about it with your teacher and fellow actors* – **teachers constantly crossed the line and 'played therapist'.** They encouraged the revealing of intimate, often horrible past experiences, secrets that then risked the actor's emotional stability in the name of acting. They might even turn to the class and ask, 'And, what about you? Have you experienced such abuse?' The class would pour forth with their stories. *It became a massive group therapy session.* Of course, when any of those actors went to recreate that torment at an audition, without the *support of their therapy group*, it generally didn't work.

I was determined to teach *only* if I had a secure grounding in psychology so I knew I would do no harm. I went back to school, earned a masters degree in clinical social work and psychotherapy. I worked in clinical settings and began to see clearly w*hat was therapy and what was actor training.* They are *two distinctly different experiences.* I feel so strongly about this that I recommend that if you are in a class where you are being asked to probe painful memories, please pretend you've just received a text from your agent telling you to leave immediately for an audition!

Along with the psychology I was learning more about *the layers of mystery in the brain itself.* A neuroscientist became my mentor and began supplying me with articles, books and guidance about advances in the field. For actors, this is invaluable. You will find in later chapters fascinating information about how your brain developed, the chemical interactions that may be making it hard for you to memorize, and a myriad other insights from the field of neuroscience.

My thirst for knowledge presented me with *many detours* but I always returned to the theatre. People have asked me how I did it all – including marriage and a family. My answer is, *'I wanted it all!'* **I am convinced that it was my willingness to take detours to study psychology and neuroscience that gave me some of the keys that are harder to find without this knowledge.**

Putting the pieces together:
Acting with passion

We'll begin with your learning how to access your Dungeon and the quest for *emotions on cue.* You'll get to know the voice in your head in a new way, as it struggles with your getting free of its demands. You'll learn about the development of your brain in the first few years of your life; how the limbic system in your brain controls so many of your behaviours. Foremost, you will begin to trust that your body has wisdom you can depend upon. You will understand how to release muscular tensions and trapped emotions. You will be learning to access your Dungeon through a series of physical cues I call *self-tuning*. You may hear some actors call it, '*Flacksing*'. Years ago an actor, leaving an *acting with passion* workshop said, 'I'm going to **Flacks** myself for that audition!' (playing off my name). It stuck and now many actors delightedly talk about *Flacksing*. Don't be confused. You may call it anything you wish!

I will be guiding you through the process of *self-tuning* where you arrive not only 'in the moment' but confident and safe that you can connect to feelings in whatever text you are speaking.

The chapters on *self-tuning* will be accompanied by a link to an online audio guide where I will talk you through the process so you can put the book down and just experience it. Ultimately you will find you can tune your instrument with amazing ease because all of it *is being absorbed on a muscular level*. The sensory cues your body experiences happen in nanoseconds. *Your muscles learn them very quickly*. You will find yourself, happily in the zone, in seconds rather than the effortful lengthy preparation most of us learned.

We are verbal animals – words resonate inside us with tremendous power. Because of that, your *self-tuning* includes not just movement and muscle release, but words that will accompany this movement. These words and phrases will be connecting to your Dungeon, *often releasing huge feelings yet not attached in any way to memory*.

There are short pieces of text for you to speak – little poems that carry universal emotions. They have no intention of reflecting your *personal experiences*, but instead offer an array of human needs and feelings. You will be astonished that some phrases will evoke big feelings and *yet on a conscious level you can't relate to them at all*. Great! You are on your way to play roles like Medea and Oedipus – I've yet to meet an actor with those autobiographies.

I will be asking you to memorize those collections of phrases because it is only through solid memorization that we get the brain interactions we need as actors. The chapter on **memorization** is filled with neuroscience that explains not only why it may be difficult for you, but offers you the secrets for releasing the neurotransmitters that will make memorizing actually easy!

I also want you to be the **consummate artist** who can meet the demands of the most challenging kinds of texts, a director who wants forty-seven takes and a production concept that means wearing wetsuits and speaking like aliens – and you are still 'in the moment'. I want you to be equally at home and connected to your Dungeon whether it's Restoration comedy or Greek tragedy.

As a superb artist you have remarkable demands on you: hitting your mark on the film set and making sure your eyes aren't wandering away from your focus point in your close-up. You have complex blocking and use of props to honour night after night, all the time in sync with your free access to feelings. You will be learning to perform the **great balancing act**, when we examine **text analysis** – its dangers and rewards, where the conscious mind and unconscious mind must work in coordination to free you to 'act with passion'.

Rehearsals, performance, critics: all opportunities to open the Dungeon and shine. Being so comfortable in your body *that movement and gesture become totally natural*, even as you adjust and move differently from character to character. When we explore **gesturing** you'll meet the amazing feedback loop between body and mind that controls your nerves and tension.

I'll be sharing many **psychological insights** from my experiences as a therapist and teacher. I promise you, *this is not to send you into therapy!* Instead, I hope it will offer you nourishing food for thought since it underscores our remarkable *human drive for health*. I will remind you that *this approach to acting is not memory-based* – trying to remember things as you read is not necessary – thought and memories will naturally occur.

Your Dungeon and all those feelings are also reading with you – they will stir and surprise you. Your biggest emotions are primal. You cannot really *remember* any of those events because they took place before they could be stored into conscious memory – just enjoy that experience.

And, of course, we will spend time together looking at the frustrating, unfair, crazy-making world of **auditions**. Casting is vital to your career and yet offers so many obstacles. I'm excited to have you try out everything in this book. Some of the ideas will make you laugh – I learned a lot of painful lessons by 'doing things wrong!' *Remember, casting is your opportunity to impress even when you are 'not right' for the role*.

Shall we begin?

I invite you to join me on this journey. I'm going to be urging you to put aside cherished myths and daring you to explore sometimes bizarre new concepts. Some of these fly in the face of all your previous training – try not to let this alarm you. **You won't lose any of the strengths you possess.** You will be *adding to and supporting your talent,* your instincts and the valuable skills you have learned.

The link online to my voice is in the *self-tuning* chapters so you can move around freely without referring to the book. Acting is an action sport. *I want you to be on your feet experiencing every new technique.* Try not to rush ahead or skip a chapter or two as you begin to enjoy the results of your *self-tuning.* I want you to have the confidence that you can trust the subtle cues you will learn as you walk towards the camera, or for your next audition.

Be ready to laugh, to love, to dream. *Unfasten your safety belt* and dare to take this ride from beginning to end. More than anything, you are *allowed to have fun.* **You might be embarking upon a great adventure!**

1
THE HOLY GRAIL: EMOTIONS ON CUE

Almost every actor shares one unique experience: the first time ever in front of an audience. You might have been seven, or twenty-seven. You went out there not knowing what would happen. Nervous, scared, probably, but your Intellect was silent. You dove in with great enthusiasm, every nerve-ending alert. You spoke your lines, laughed or cried and the *audience loved you!* After just that *one* time we all said, 'I want more! I want to do this again!' And so we became actors.

You wanted to experience that joy again and *you wanted to do this thing you loved really well.*

You worked with actors who knew more than you – so much to learn. You studied. You dedicated yourself. But then, all of a sudden, you found that the exhilarating joy you had felt at first *was being replaced with anxiety, tension and a feeling that you were working too hard.* What happened? For far too many actors the process of training 'to be an actor' becomes the process of diminished confidence and raging self-doubt.

When actors tell me about their frustrations they talk about 'excessive effort' and the feeling that they are acting 'from the neck up', always 'watching themselves'. Yes, that's the evidence. The Intellect began to assert itself, telling you what you should or should not be doing; *constantly judging, criticizing, 'directing' and often paralysing.* The state of aliveness became elusive. Where did it go?

The voice in the head: The Intellect

What a tyrant. Odd that you didn't hear the Intellect that first time onstage. Did it grow out of nowhere? Absolutely not. It's an old friend and quite familiar to you. You've heard it all your life. For years it has been the voice of *caution and fear of failure*, generally telling you others are more capable than you are. It has been with you throughout your education no matter what you chose to study. No one escapes that critical voice. In acting it seems to bloom full force.

The more training you receive as an actor the more ammunition this voice seems to get – more ways to punish you: 'not real, not truthful, not funny, not exciting, not sexy, not interesting, or simply *not good enough*'. Do you want me to go on?

The quest for emotions on cue, entry into the Dungeon and escape from the Intellect is the heart and soul of *acting with passion*. From time to time, you have one of those wonderful rehearsals or performances where the voice is still, but you can't be *sure* it will happen again. When your director says, 'Great. Now tomorrow, I want the *same* thing,' it's the kiss of death!

You can't possibly repeat what you just did because *you have no idea how it happened* or what actually took place. You remember the sense of aliveness, but that moment-to-moment *replay* your brain usually gives you isn't there. The Intellect must have been taking a nap.

When you go to recreate that last rehearsal, trying to remember what you did, you are once again in the grips of the constant direction and feedback from your head. Your familiar rehearsal companions have returned: effort, tension, pushing feelings, being physically tight, being totally in your head and utterly exhausted. Your director exclaims, *'Oh, no! You are intellectualizing again!'*

Acting with Passion is your voyage into the wondrous ways we will escape the tyranny of the Intellect. First I will share the most important fact. **The Intellect *never* tells the truth.** Yes. It is filling your head with *lies*. I can hear you arguing with me already: 'But sometimes it tells me how well I'm doing.' My answer: don't trust it. You may indeed be doing very well, but the Intellect's approval often comes before pulling the rug out from under your feet. Or, it can tell you to make an emotion *bigger* – leading you to *churn those feelings* and then applauding all the effort. The Intellect has its own agenda: one that is seldom in your best interest.

The Intellect/access to feelings conundrum!

One thing all actors sense is that there seems to be a connection between the Intellect – being 'in your head' – and the *inability to call up feelings* with ease. Emotions are the actor's stock-in-trade. It's as though there is an unwritten contract between audience and actors – actors are paid to express feelings in order to kindle emotions in the audience. It is *expected* that actors will make an audience laugh, cry, feel joy, anger, heartbreak – a big responsibility.

Even experienced professional actors talk about the horrible pressure when they *need* to express a certain feeling that it won't be there. The torture when the playwright puts in brackets *sobbing hysterically*; or when the next line is, 'Please stop crying.' These are invitations to your Intellect to keep reminding you that you must *produce those tears on cue.*

This 'holy grail' is central to Stanislavski's work. His technique of *emotional recall* has been widely embraced as the answer. You *need* tears. You remember a sad event; the memory sparks instant emotion. Your eyes might fill with tears at the remembrance. But then a problem arises when you need to repeat this take after take, or eight performances a week.

Many people don't realize that Stanislavski himself rejected this technique late in his life. He saw actors turning themselves inside out trying to force memories into emotions. Before he died he was exploring other avenues – one of them was working physically.

But for most of us Stanislavski's concepts came to us via the Method – the creation primarily of Lee Strasburg and the Actors Studio. Many teachers adopted the Method and evolved their own variations on *emotional recall*, like the *Magic If* and *What If?* All of these techniques became anointed as the purest way to emotional truth onstage. I know I wasn't the only one remembering and replaying past hurts and cruelties, *hoping* those feelings would sharpen and be available when needed. There are actors who do succeed in locking in these feelings for future use. But, in truth, *most* find this a hit or miss experience.

The 'What If?' or 'Magic If' actors create *fictional scenarios*, some of which include imagining horrible pain being visited on a loved one: a war, a flood, an automobile accident. The purpose of these efforts is to produce feelings and often to create an emotional connection to events in a play that have no apparent resonance with personal experience. Sometimes, the creation of the fiction is so exciting it seems to work wonders. But no matter how effective those thoughts might be the *first time*, they seem to *lose their potency* very quickly.

(One of the sad side-effects of these techniques, if actors become *skilful* at creating these scenarios of death and heartbreak, is the *guilt* they must carry for *using* their loved ones. Feeling that they are betraying sacred memories or even causing *possible harm* because of these fantasies.)

Why is it that these techniques aren't dependable and don't always produce the same state of aliveness they did the first time? There are things happening at a brain level that can undermine all our determined efforts.

All of these techniques come up against a powerful brain mechanism: Desensitization

I told you how multi-layered and complex our minds are. This is a perfect example. One of our hallmark abilities as human beings is the ability to learn new things. *Desensitization* is one of the amazing ways in which the brain makes it possible to overcome fear to try new, difficult or challenging behaviours. The first time we try something unknown we might bring a great deal of fear and anxiety to the task, but each time the task is repeated the fear level diminishes. You can see that without this capacity we would never have learned to do anything new.

Nowadays we mainly hear the term *desensitization* used in a psychotherapy context – a technique for helping people to get over phobias. It works like this: therapists guide a patient through *the repetition of a feared action or thought* until the brain has successfully *diminished the fear, and the potency of the imagined danger*, by utilizing this invaluable brain resource.

You can see immediately how this *instinctive* process, however, would undermine the strength of a powerful memory or imagined scenario once you repeat it a few times. Those of you who have been frustrated with these various forms of *emotional recall*, probably blaming yourself for not doing them correctly, have simply experienced your mind's protective mechanism of desensitization.

To me, the most destructive result of desensitization has been the belief that unearthing *new fresh* painful memories or fantasies is therefore the only answer. Actors are encouraged to *cannibalize* their lives. When remembering the death of your dear cat fails, you think, 'I'll remember when my grandmother died.'

This approach has led to a cult that celebrates actors constantly in the grips of pain, anger or high emotion. *If they are self-destructive or living in a dysfunctional relationship, acting teachers indirectly imply this makes them more exciting onstage.* If you live with an alcoholic who abuses you, wow! You've won the brass ring. You have *endless* painful material to draw on.

The brain's other issues with emotional recall

There are other issues beyond desensitization at work that make these very popular acting techniques less *dependable* than we were led to believe. All of these techniques share one fact. They are created via *thought*. That means the effort must be triggered in the *language centre of the brain*.

1 'I'll remember when my cat, Muffy, died.' Whether I embellish the scene with the time of day, the colour of the chair I was sitting in, or just go straight to Muffy, I am using my 'story writing' mind to create this memory as I call up these details. This part of the brain *immediately alerts the Intellect.* What a dilemma. The Intellect, full of judgement, monitors the images and your responses – e.g. 'Emotion not coming quickly enough. Image unclear, or wrong image.'

2 The second pitfall is that a memory or an imagined story immediately requires the *visual cortex* to provide the images needed. Therein lies a *huge* problem. The visual cortex is a very busy place in your head. It consumes a massive amount of *brain real estate*. You can get an idea of just how dominant the visual is when you look at the drawing of the brain. It's fast and constantly active. Because of this it gets *bored* very quickly. Think how rapidly you *change the remote control* of your television. Channel surfing is your visual cortex saying, 'boring!' within microseconds.

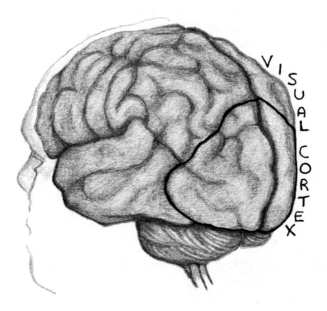

3 It has been approximated that the visual brain gets bored after a *seventeenth of a second*. Any image you give it will fade and dissolve within a breath or two – to hold onto an image takes *great effort*. You've noticed that, haven't you? There's sweet Muffy, all furry and brown, big eyes, whiskers, and then, poof! She's gone. 'Muffy, come back. Please, I need you to help me feel sad!'

4 Some acting classes suggest the solution is spending *more time* creating detailed visualizations, supposedly imprinting them in your brain so you can call upon them when needed. This requires great determination and hard work in trying to sustain these images; trying to make them 'real'. Just remember, if you begin *really seeing things that don't exist*, that's called hallucinating – clinically quite serious.

We will revisit the thorny issue of visualization as a staple of most actors' core skills. For now, just think about this: when Madame Ranevskaya says, 'Oh, my beautiful cherry orchard,' the same visual brain challenges are there.

With these three forces – desensitization, language centre/Intellect, and visual cortex boredom – no wonder so many actors struggle to access feelings with these techniques.

There is an alternative path

What if you could find an *endless supply of emotions* without having to 'think' about it? What would happen if, in fact, the *body* contained its own memories, having locked away emotions in your muscles? What if it is almost *impossible to think* your way into *many* of these feelings because you don't actually have *conscious knowledge* of them?

When we look at the way the body and brain are wired we see that there are networks of connections between our emotions and our bodies. Eighty per cent of our neurons are found *outside* of the brain and nervous system. Huge numbers of them are found in the stomach (enteric nervous system.) The stomach is one of the body's main producers of serotonin – the neurotransmitter so important in regulating moods and emotions.

To have a concept of how recent most of the discoveries are, in the early twentieth century the idea that the body and mind were completely separate was never questioned. For me, the 'Eureka' moment must have been when Reich, working with Freud, began to observe his patients' bodies. I imagine the scene when he said one day, 'So, Sigmund, what about the body?' At which point Freud, being a prudish Austrian of his period answered, 'I don't want to talk about the body!' And thus the two geniuses parted ways.

This controversy has not abated even as it appears we have more scientific evidence. If you chat with enough people about these ideas today, you'll hear someone quote famous neuroscientists who think all the things I believe are nonsense. They will tell you there are no 'definitive' answers. Neuroscience has many more discoveries for the future.

Reich went on to create the framework for much of the mind-body psychology that is woven into the fabric of our modern lives – holistic medicine, psychosomatic illness, alternative healing through touch. His theory was that the *chronic tensions* and *body postures* he observed in his patients represented *feelings* deeply buried within their muscles. He called this chronic tightness, 'armour'. His most famous disciple, Alexander Lowen, created a form of therapy called bioenergetics, which recommended specific movements to release these muscular tensions, breaking down the armour, thus releasing emotions and *deeply buried memories*.

(Any of you who do yoga, as I do, realize that this mind-body connection was known 5,000 years ago, and pervades all Eastern philosophy!)

What sparked *my* interest as an actor and then working with patients as a therapist was the possibility that I might find a *pathway other than conscious memory for accessing feelings*. I grew confident that emotions are *visceral* rather than intellectual. Building on Reich's identification of the *different areas* of the body as holding particular feelings, I developed the *acting with passion* approach.

Emotions throughout your body

In 1988 Candace Pert's research, beautifully detailed in her book, *Molecules of Emotion*, was the first to identify *opiate receptors* throughout the body. These are the molecules of emotion found in the immune system, richly in the stomach, everywhere in the body. **She had proved the mind-body connection.** Till then, the assumption had been that opiate receptors only dwelled in the brain. The neuroscience world went into upheaval. This was revolutionary. Since then, more and more research has identified this connection. Reich's intuition was correct. Somehow, the body and brain are connected.

Reich liked to focus on specific parts of the body as holding, uniquely, certain emotions. *I have not found this to be so rigidly true.* We are infinitely more complicated than that. Remember we have emotion receptors everywhere in our bodies – in our skin as well. I will explain these areas in broad brush strokes, however, as we will be exploring them together in much greater detail as you experience them physically.

The chest

The chest, shoulders, neck and head alignment hold sadness, grief and disappointment. This is the tightness you recognize when you are deeply upset. After a particularly difficult day you walk into your home feeling as though you are carrying an anvil on your chest. You see someone walking down the street, shoulders tight, chest withdrawn and sunken, and instinctively you say, 'That person looks miserable.'

The stomach

Your *youngest* feelings – fear, fear of abandonment, fear of rejection, fear for your life – live in your stomach. I laugh as I think of how we actors decide to call our agent and then immediately have to go to the toilet. The thoughts arise, 'My agent doesn't love me. Will he think I'm a pest? He hasn't called in three months, maybe he'll be angry if I bother him?' And so the stomach muscles cramp with fear of rejection. These feelings seem to come directly from the limbic system which we will discuss in detail later on.

The hands

Our hands are all about *needs* and *communicating our needs*. They seem to hold unique muscular memory. The pre-verbal period of infancy appears to be imprinted in the hands – in terms of our 'animal species' *this is a precarious survival period*. Our hands spoke volumes before we had words to say. By three months a baby's hands reach out into the world to touch, grab and most importantly to ask for *vital needs to be met*. The hands ask for love by grasping and signalling for attention. Before your first words were formed your hands were 'speaking' constantly. Incredibly important for actors is this strong connection our hands have to words and the language centre of the brain.

The face, jaw and throat

Facial tension is all about hiding *real* feelings. Children learn very early on to 'wipe that expression off their face'. *They become little actors.* They learn to hide how they really feel. The eyes and particularly the mouth, throat and jaw have been trained to suppress screams, tears and rebellion. You can understand how these tensions are perilous for actors. The throat muscles had to learn to hold back tears and shouting – all the feelings we were taught to control because they were *socially unacceptable impulses*. We needed to learn to substitute words instead. We learned to say 'please' and 'thank you'. This did not happen without a great deal of struggle. The tensions actors battle in freeing their voices are a reflection of this early formative period affecting the delicate muscles in the throat and jaw. *The muscles around the eyes develop the ability to hold back tears.* We all learned *to wear a mask*.

The pelvis

The pelvis obviously holds sexuality; less obviously, it holds powerful rage. It holds some of our most primitive urges – to protect, to fight back, to assert, to avenge, to conquer. Those feelings link us directly to our evolutionary roots and our *instinct to survive*. Survival often meant protecting our 'territory' or the difference between having enough to eat and starving to death. This connects our pelvis to deep wells of anger, aggression, willingness to fight and kill. When actors release the muscles that control the movement of the pelvis they experience surges of energy and power.

Visit the zoo one day and watch our ancestors – the chimps and the baboons. You will see through their play and protection of territory how the pelvis constantly moves to assert, to threaten: 'I'm bigger and stronger than you. Give me that banana, or else.' They look like Al

Capone gangsters with each aggressive forward thrust of the pelvis, as in the classic 'Fuck you!'

Understanding the role the pelvis plays, you can see how the legs, especially the thighs, knees and feet, can become rigid. They are among the many muscles trying to suppress the anger.

Isn't muscular tension a fact of life? Why not just relax?

The idea that actors struggle with tension is certainly not new. Every acting student has been guided through many relaxation processes. Muscles are asked to relax progressively. Actors lie down, breathe deeply and, for the most part, feel really great. The main problem, other than this being pretty time-consuming, is that there doesn't seem to be much carry-over into actual performance.

More troubling to me and to many movement teachers – clearly also in the mind-body world – is that the 'relaxed state' is really not the same as being in 'a state of aliveness'. In life we would seem to be zombies if we walked around with the level of deep relaxation we've been encouraged to practise. Feeling 'mellow' and 'oh, so calm' would not be the kind of energy you would want to embark on a madcap farce like *A Comedy of Errors*.

In addition, as I began my journey, learning to move muscles *purposefully to release feelings*, I noticed how different classic *relaxation* is. Not just that it would evaporate the moment someone went onstage. But it seemed to almost make for *more tension onstage*. As if all of the *chronic tensions* reappeared almost instantly. It became obvious that performance tension was something that could not be controlled through *mentally guided relaxation*.

The chronic tensions are those we've developed through suppression of feelings. We've lived with them for so many years that we are almost completely *unaware of them*. However, the stress of performance and the fear of failure sets a *cascade in motion*. The *habitual tensions* communicate with *all of the other muscles* in the body. They, in turn, pick up the danger signals and tighten – hence, giving the impression to actors that the problem is *generalized* tension.

Why do we develop this muscular tension Reich called 'armour?'

I'm going to start at the beginning, the day you were born. At birth you are still 'a work in progress'. Your brain is awaiting the massive input that will create much of your personality. You have billions of neurons just waiting to be assigned jobs that will determine how your cerebral real estate is parcelled out.

You do have one part of your brain, however, that is *hard-wired*. This is the limbic system, located in the centre of your brain, one of the most ancient in evolutionary terms. It is almost identical to all other mammals on earth. This is where *all of your primal drives and instincts for survival dwell* – these are activated even before your birth. We are a unique species in that our young are dependent for years. Deep within your DNA and limbic system, therefore, is the knowledge that without those adults who hold you and feed you, *you would die*. A lion cub at six months can hunt and defend its territory. At six months if you were put out on a doorstep, you would perish within days. This fact has profound repercussions.

I am setting the stage for you to understand how it could be possible that you have a vast well of emotions and you may have no idea where they came from. The crazy, illogical feelings we all carry around are rooted in this murky early time *before we could speak*. We have no *conscious memories* of those early years even though it was then that we laid down much of the blueprint for who we would become.

Your brain was incredibly busy in your first few years. Although your limbic system is hard-wired, a great deal of your *cortex and prefrontal cortex* – responsible for planning and complex cognitive behaviour – is like a blank slate. Unlike other animals on earth *you* must fit into a culture, a family and a society speaking a complex language.

Those first years you needed to learn over 100,000 words. The sounds unique to the language or languages you learned would shape the *auditory pathways* in your brain and even the *neuromuscular connections in your mouth, jaw and tongue*. Your colour perception and visual orientation would be influenced by the sights and shapes surrounding you. You would learn to recognize

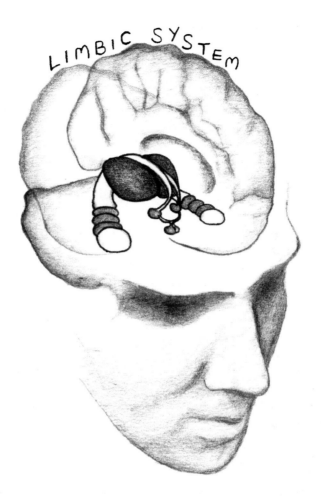

your native music as *pleasant* and to find another culture's music *incomprehensible*. You were learning to be part of a specific culture and society.

In order to fit into that social structure your family, *particularly your parents*, had the incredibly difficult task of civilizing you. Adorable infants are actually *primitive savage creatures* – responding to the survival drives of the limbic system. Babies cry out the minute they wake up and demand instant attention. If that first cry fails to rouse someone the infant is consumed with fierce anger, face turning red, fists tightened

– expressing pure animal rage. Its primal urges are screaming, 'If you don't rescue me I'll die!'

When not demanding instant attention, the baby is grabbing anything nearby, greedily putting it in his mouth, sucking or biting – satisfying other primitive urges. Infants and small children have a huge repertoire of *'socially unacceptable behaviours'* – totally natural, of course. But, nonetheless, needing to be corrected at some point.

Can you imagine what would have happened to any of us had a parent *not* taught us to control those behaviours? If not, if you are sitting next to someone right now and feeling a little bored, you would probably lean over and bite them on the shoulder. It feels good to bite! There isn't anything much more satisfying to a two-year-old than biting someone. You had to be *taught not to do this*, however. And it's a good thing you learned to restrain that powerful impulse.

All of the things that have taught us not to express emotions beyond our society's norms came from painful lessons: learning to postpone gratification, to hold back babyish tears, to stop screaming with rage, to say, 'I love you', when we really wanted to say, 'I hate you'.

And to make this journey even more complicated, the people teaching us to do all of these difficult, unpleasant tasks were the people on whom we *depended for our survival*. That survival was predicated on love. As long as they loved us we would not be abandoned. In return we learned to love them. We will come back to this thorny issue as it plays a key role in shaping our emotions.

For now, imagine you are only three and it's the *second time* you have pinched your baby brother. The first time was met with mild disapproval and a reprimand not to do it again. This time you look up and see anger on the face of your parent. *Anger and rejection!* 'Bad little boy! Leave the room until you can behave yourself.' Everything inside you – your survival DNA depending on that very person – is crying out. 'NO! Please don't reject me! I'll die.' This desperation triggers rage for being made to feel so miserable. You are awash with huge conflicting feelings. You might throw yourself on the floor sobbing or kicking or begging for forgiveness. Over time, however, you learned to master all of these volcanic *feelings through the tightening of various muscles.*

This is how your armour was constructed. You were learning, on a *muscular level* to control your emotions, how to be polite and hide real feelings. Let's observe that three-year-old working at not bursting into tears or having a tantrum, and instead mumbling, 'I'm sorry. I *love* my baby brother.'

You will instantly see the *huge effort he makes in his jaw*. It will be clenched so tightly it will probably tremble, as will his lips. Sometimes you might even be aware of his teeth chattering. The muscles around his eyes will look tight, his eyebrows tensed. *The muscles in his throat* will be working very hard as well, even though you can't see them. Do you remember that feeling of having 'a lump in your throat' when you were sitting in school willing yourself not to cry? That was the action of your *swallowing muscles* clamping down to prevent you from sobbing.

If you look at the body of this frightened, unhappy child you will see that his knees have probably locked, his hips and pelvis have become rigid, and his chest tight and withdrawn. The stomach muscles are clenched. His body is experiencing a whole repertoire of muscular tension. With frequent repetition of these patterns the muscles begin to build those tensions into muscle memory. This is not muscle memory as we think of it – having to do with various forms of exercise *educating* muscles. **Instead, what appears to happen is that the muscles *habituate*.** Those layers of tightening simply start to *feel normal*. Even the slightest signal of rejection can set them in motion.

In describing this single scene you can begin to understand that we are dealing with a whole network of muscles that interact and feed signals to each other. The tightening of the tiny muscles beneath the eyes – I call them the *bravery muscles* – is involved in teaching us to hold back tears. For little boys, what treacherous territory they must cover to learn to be 'men'. Was there anything more humiliating than being called a 'cry baby'? For some actors those muscles became so alert with bravery that they can feel the tears start in their eyes and *never spill*. What brilliant iron control. Probably developed by the time you were four.

When the bravery muscles are recruited, for boys and girls, they are communicating with the muscles in the throat. These are busy tightening to prevent full-fledged crying. The jaw, a strong, large bone and hinge, is attached to muscles leading into the neck, along the cheeks, encompassing the mouth. No wonder doing an on-camera audition can be such disaster. The fear of failure raging in the brain sets off this cascade of muscular tension in the face.

Our work is to *dismantle this tension*, not by telling the muscles to relax, but instead by *embracing* their underlying desire to express feelings.

The next step: Expressing feelings through text

I hope you are excited about the prospect of finding all these body connections *dwelling in your unconscious mind*. Your magic entry, surprisingly however, is through deeply memorized text. Yes, you read that correctly. Let me explain why before you glare daggers at me! It seems I offer emotional freedom and then I want to talk about learning lines!

The muscular tension we will be exploring in this book, developed early in your life, was to *suppress the expression* of feelings. As you became more and more verbal, these feelings soon *attached themselves to words*. Many of those words never got a chance to be spoken. **The only way to completely *bypass the Intellect* is to permit your emotions to connect to words *safely embedded in your deep memory storage* – where they can interact directly with the complex illogic of your unconscious.** You know, from personal experience, that when you have a monologue or play really solidly memorized, how free you feel and the remarkable new associations to the text you can make.

This is the trick of how you are wired. It appears that really deeply memorized text is stored in a *different part of the brain than the 'almost memorized'* we are more accustomed to. With this deep storage we can get immediate entry into the Dungeon.

What a gift to be an actor! Your feelings are just waiting to be heard, waiting to be *given a voice*. You work with texts where writers offer you words of richness and power. Don't short change yourself by going for the superficial feelings available when reading or half-memorizing. *Those words need to live in your body!* All this means they *must be memorized well*. If you are one of the many actors who hate memorizing, you are in for some surprises! It may not be as hard as you think.

The next chapter, called *Memorization: a fresh look and no whinging, please*, will guide you through some surprising brain research that I believe makes memorizing *much easier*. At the end of the chapter you will find very short pieces to learn, *written to offer you access to feelings*. Please, *also work on some monologues that you find appealing and challenging*. Learn them while experimenting with the techniques described in the next chapter. **It's time for us to move on so you can begin learning those lines!**

2
MEMORIZATION: A FRESH LOOK AND NO WHINGING, PLEASE

Why begin with memorization? Isn't this a book about acting?
The actors in Shakespeare's company performed over 150 plays each year. They were clearly memorizing machines. That skill was crucial to their success.

Acting with passion offers you the gateway to connecting emotionally with the words of your text *via the body instead of the head*. This means, however, that you must take memorization as seriously as Shakespeare's company did. It demands that you learn lines, and learn them *thoroughly*. If part of your brain (the conscious mind) is searching for the next word it is much harder to access emotions (residing in the unconscious). Almost every other approach to acting puts much less emphasis on this skill. It is often only at *crunch time*, soon to face an audience, that actors are expected to know their lines.

More specifically, in order to get value from the exercises in this book, you will need lines you can speak effortlessly. Every new concept you learn you will test out with *memorized* text.

Will this really help me to 'act with passion'?

The heart of the issue, as an actor, is the ease in accessing emotions – in the moment, *every* moment. Then why do I place so much importance on memorization? 'That's not acting!' you say. But wait.

Acting is a complex art form – it depends upon many systems working *together* seamlessly. One of them is the brain's ability to call up lines from memory (prefrontal cortex) at the same time as the body is moving (motor cortex), possibly hitting a mark on the film set (spatial recognition), while emotions are surging (limbic system/amygdala), and much more. All of that coordination takes place, for the most part, in the smooth balance of our unconscious and conscious minds. That's why I call the Intellect 'the enemy' – the more you are in the grip of your Intellect the less access you have to your mysterious unconscious and the easy interplay of so many different brain/body systems.

The kind of moment-to-moment aliveness I want you to achieve means the quieting of your Intellect and accessing your Dungeon. With that comes the relief of not hearing the running commentary of your Intellect. This is a double-edged sword however – **if you want that Intellect to be quiet, you cannot call upon it to help you remember the next word or phrase**. As soon as memory falters, the Intellect gears up. Along with helping you to find the next word comes the usual barrage of, *'You are hopeless! You don't know your lines. You can't act.'* How impossible does being 'in the moment' feel *then*?

You know from experience that the moment you 'dry' you can feel your *body shift into tension*. Remember for a moment one of those agonizing searches for a line that felt like ten minutes (probably no more than a few seconds). Can you recall the physical paralysis that probably set in? You were communicating with all your armour, tightening those muscles as well. I am convinced that emotional access, physical ease and deep memory storage are all *interconnected in the unconscious mind*. **The discipline of superb memorization is your entry key into your richest inner resource – by knowing material inside out your Intellect stays quiet.**

Connecting to a text happens in the unconscious

In the next chapters you will be finding ways to access the pathway that begins deep in the muscles of your body leading directly to your store of full, wonderful, illogical feelings. You will find the joy of discovering *how your unique inner world can illuminate a text* as you've never dreamed!

Your Dungeon is not a place of logic. It is rich with feelings, many of them not making sense in your conscious mind.

A few years ago I worked with an actor who was playing Oberon in *A Midsummer Night's Dream*. After our mind-body release he did a very emotional speech and wondered if he could try one of Oberon's. This is a character who has magnificent poetry but isn't usually played as deeply emotional.

He started one of the speeches.

Thou rememberest when once I sat upon a promontory . . .

He spoke simply and clearly. His body was alive and open to feelings so when he got to . . .

Mark'd I where the bolt of Cupid fell;
It fell upon a little western flower
Before milk-white, now purple with love's wound.

. . . as he said the word 'purple' *his eyes filled with tears*. While the tears were rolling down his cheeks he spoke the rest of the speech filled with sadness. When he finished, the actors in the class asked, 'What were you *thinking* when you said, *purple*?' He said, 'I have no idea. I don't even *like* the colour purple! But now, for the first time I understand how much he loves Titania and how much this trick costs him.' *Those are the kinds of delicious, illogical, beyond-our-conscious-knowledge* connections to text that make each actor so excitingly unique!

The goal is to connect with your text emotionally, not intellectually. Once you have lines solid and the body free and alive, you will find that your emotions spark with the words instantly. Remember, we are *verbal* animals. We don't bark or neigh or chirp. We use words. *They are deeply enmeshed in our earliest experiences and in our every feeling.*

It's not as though your unconscious mind/Dungeon is asleep till you access it. No, it is alert all the time. In fact, your unconscious mind is reading this book along with you and your Intellect. It has many words and *connections to words* that spark feelings you didn't know you possessed.

Actors, using these techniques, are always amazed at how *easy* it is to discover emotions, no matter how unexpected, that seem so right and true for the text, especially after years of trying to *decide* what emotion they want to feel and then trying to produce it. That's because when emotions are *stirred by the words* rather than being 'directed' by the Intellect they seem to come from our deepest truth. We will be discussing the complicated issue of text analysis later on. But for now, if it leads you to decide, 'the character is angry here, then sad here and desperate there', you will find it almost impossible to impose these directions on your Dungeon. In fact, your Intellect will make sure you can't. You will experience this very quickly as we move into our exploration of your mind-body connections in the next chapter. But first, we must take a closer look at this thing so many of you seem to dread: memorization!

How your previous training might have handled this task and shaped your thinking

Let's step back for a moment and look at what you have previously experienced in your training. In many classes or rehearsals the script is first and foremost the *springboard for a great deal of creative thought*. The fact that the actors will have to perform these lines from memory is hardly mentioned. Actors begin with analysis, scouring the script for *meaning*. They might analyze given circumstances. Or ponder needs, goals and objectives for their character. They comb the script for psychology and feelings. Actors also explore the character, often doing animal work or improvisations to get to know their character's past history and own it. They are sometimes encouraged to create inner monologues, mining the concept of subtext, creating a 'back-story' that might explain motivation for this or that action. All this can be great fun. Actors feel alive and creative in these explorations. They can undoubtedly enrich the actor's understanding of the play and character. However, bottom line, **they *postpone* the less appealing task of learning the lines and in doing so indirectly *undervalue* it**.

I am not saying that understanding the text is a problem. Of course, it is necessary. But it shouldn't be *a substitute* for learning lines. After script analysis and backstory work, the next postponement of learning lines comes with rehearsing while holding the script. This approach may help you become *familiar* with the text, but since the *focus is on acting*, the brain is not geared up to *memorize*. (Which requires a certain amount of pure repetition.)

The main issue we must face is that when we *read we are using a different part of the brain* than when retrieving words from long-term memory storage. It is this *essential difference in brain processing* that has driven my belief that memorization *the earlier the better* is more vital than most people seem to think.

Acting with passion offers a different journey in the actor's relationship to text. Because of the way the brain processes words in memory, so very much can be discovered *only* after lines are learned – insights and connections that I believe are infinitely more satisfying to an actor. Think about how much you enjoy the third and fourth week of a run when lines are finally secure. Aren't you amazed at the discoveries you make? How often have you wished you could have opened *then*?

I had a very lively discussion with a group of young directors when I was teaching classes in Israel. They were horrified to learn that when I direct I ask actors to come to the first rehearsal with lines learned. They explained their rehearsal process. Grounded in the Moscow Art Theatre of Stanislavski by the founding members of Israeli theatre during the country's inception, theatre companies traditionally have long rehearsal periods. Sometimes as long as three or four months. My delighted question was, 'So that means that when you are doing final run-throughs before tech week the lines are rock solid!' They looked at me bewildered. 'No. The lines are often shaky even close to opening night.' All the improvisations, the character analysis, the games, the relaxation, the chanting, had not produced *organically* learned lines. I think it's time we looked at what needs to happen at a *brain level* to achieve the confidence that your text is secure.

Why is it so hard? A look at what the brain is doing

It's a fair question when you see that *the brain was actually designed to memorize*. Look at all the words, grammar, syntax you had to learn in those first few years – thousands and thousands of words. You spent your first years essentially *memorizing everything* with a great deal of ease. You learned numbers, letters, colours, the names of animals, people, objects – tree, house, doll, kite, Aunt Susan and Cousin Harry. You learned poems and songs. You memorized books that were read to you by adults over and over. And happily you went off to school to learn more.

Unfortunately, *many of us encountered a crisis that made memorization much harder.* Around the age of seven or eight there are two events that usually take place almost simultaneously. **Developmental psychologists tell us that this is the time when the psyche learns 'self consciousness'.** In the earliest years children see themselves as the centre of the universe with everyone an extension of them. Later on they understand their 'separateness' but have not yet developed a great deal of 'self-observation'. By eight years we have all begun to experience a *sense of our selves* that includes our fear of failure. We get embarrassed. We are aware that we make mistakes. We feel isolated. We wonder if everyone else might find this or that task easy, yet for us it is difficult – maybe they are all 'better at it'.

So, we have entered the age where it is *normal to feel self-consciousness* when we stand up in front of fellow classmates. We feel humiliation if we make a mistake. We hear our own voice and it sounds wrong. We sense our body and how stiff and awkward it has become. We see others looking at us and feel their judgement. Into this psychological storm enters our teacher. She means well. She believes she is advancing our education as she says sweetly, 'Now boys and girls, I'm going to ask you to do something *very difficult*. You will ask your mummies and daddies to help you. I'm going to pass out a poem for you to *learn by heart*. Yes, you will *memorize* this and say every word correctly. Then you will recite it in *front of the class*.'

Thank you, well-meaning teacher. In one little assignment *she has taken the glorious ability your brain possesses to learn things effortlessly, and she has called it difficult.* She's also *paired it with the self-consciousness* you will experience when you stand up to recite this poem. If you were one of the many people for whom this was an excruciating experience, no wonder you groan at the idea of having to learn lines.

Our job is to unhook that wretched event and its reverberations. 'I'm not good at memorizing. I must be stupid. This is so hard for me. I work at it and I still can't get it.' Remember, your brain was *designed to memorize. It's an electrical and chemical process*. We need to get your neurons charged, your neurotransmitters flowing and your synapses firing. And you can do that!

It is recognized that fear is invaluable for *learning things connected to survival*, but *counterproductive* when it comes to higher brain functions that involve language. The moment you feel fear, anxiety, threat, your body responds with the classic 'fight or flight' reaction to danger.

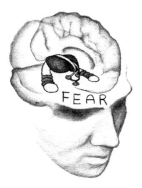

Your eyes see a tiger approaching. Instantly your brain registers, 'Danger!' **However, the brain is incredibly efficient.** Systems are recruited for survival and *systems unneeded are basically shut down*. Learning a new monologue would be absurd as that tiger approaches. The action part of the brain is fed glucose to heighten alertness and rapid response, neurotransmitters surge. Any brain system not organized to grapple with survival is put *on hold – those neurotransmitters kept to a minimum*. Wouldn't it be silly to feed the parts of the brain needed to memorize *Hamlet*? Instead, you need to be thinking, 'I'll climb that hill. Dive into that cave. Pick up my spear. Run.'

Now let's go back to our dear childhood teacher. The recitation of the poem was a disaster. The class giggled when you stumbled on a word and then you went totally blank. Your brain/body was in full-fledged 'fight or flight' mode. If you could have run for a hill you would have done so gladly. *Unconsciously you were learning a harsh lesson*: 'I am a failure at this task. Danger!'

Fast forward. You become an actor and you guard your guilty secret – you hate and *fear* memorizing lines. You are cast in a lovely role and it's time to learn the lines. *Your anxiety level rises and your brain shifts into that survival mode*, convinced this is an impossible task and you will fail. It becomes almost impossible to get the words to stick because your brain has shut down the memorization avenues and reduced the flow of neurotransmitters. Then memorizing becomes very hard. You can't get anything to stick. Awful!

This cycle is made even worse if you happen to be dyslexic. Over the years I have worked with many talented dyslexic actors. I remind them that there is exciting research showing that *this brain anomaly is linked to rich creative gifts*. But ease of memorization is not one of them. Dyslexics all seem to carry wounds that have been inflicted by teachers who have berated and diminished them. The techniques I'm outlining seem to be quite effective, as they directly target the paralysing fear and offer a brain-friendly alternative.

The body holds the key

Fortunately, we are just dealing with the release of chemicals and electrical firing of neurons, *we're not dealing with some hard-wired inadequacy*. You can become very skilled at memorization. You just need to learn the techniques.

There is exciting recent research that confirms a connection between the motor cortex, emotions and memory. We will be building upon this remarkable aspect of the interplay between body and mind. The body is constantly sending messages to the brain about our well-being and our safety. The brain can't really 'see' the body. It senses it based on how much brain territory various parts of the body take up.

We must learn to send a message to the brain that will tell it we are not under threat and therefore can permit the mind to focus on other things – learning, memorizing. Sending this message is incredibly easy. Researchers found that when people moved *in habitual non-threatened ways* – doing exercise, making a bed, fixing a meal, folding laundry –

the 'fight or flight' state eased and they were able to memorize more easily. *The brain seemed to say, ' We must be okay since the body is no longer on alert.'*
This is because there is a feedback loop from body to brain.
This is a powerful mechanism, vital to our well-being. As an actor you will learn to count on this *feedback loop* to let you move with ease, think with ease, memorize with ease and access your Dungeon and emotions with ease. It is amazingly straightforward: *the tighter the body becomes with fear the more it signals the brain to ramp up with more defence* – getting even tighter – then you are in a completely defensive, pure survival mode. *The more the body moves in non-defensive ways, open arms and chest, not a hint of response to danger* – the more quickly the feedback loop reverses and the brain says, 'We must not be under attack. All systems back to normal.' Think about how much less complicated this is than berating yourself for your anxiety. Telling yourself not to be stressed is useless!

Have you ever found yourself *pacing* when you memorize? It's your *instinct* kicking in. Those movements are cuing your brain. The more active, *comfortable and normal your movement*, the easier it becomes to signal the brain that the danger has passed. Your pacing begins to release the needed neurotransmitters. It has also been found that the more vigorous the movement, the more vigorous the flow of neurotransmitters. And that extra energy uses and dissipates the adrenaline of fear.

There is some fascinating research taking place as I write this book led by a psychiatrist, Dr John Ratey at Harvard Medical School, demonstrating how more intense movement affects the hippocampus and therefore the whole 'learning process'. He has collected some pretty convincing data that *aerobic exercise* – specifically running for at least a half hour – releases the perfect brain chemistry needed for learning. If you are interested in testing this 'bleeding edge' research, *try memorizing during and after a half-hour run*.

The hands-language centre connection

Another piece in this mind-body puzzle has to do with the hands. On brain scans one can see that the movement of the hands appears to be directly connected to the language centre in the brain. Simple observation tells us how often we see ourselves moving our fingers and hands as we're saying, 'It's on the tip of my tongue. I know that word . . . it just won't come.' Sometimes the fingers almost seem to be leafing through a dictionary in space while we search for a word.

Would you like to see how the brain actually perceives the body? As you will notice in the drawing of the homunculus – the neuroscience name for the way the brain actually 'sees' the body, the hands are enormous. This reflects their close connection to cognition on many levels. They carry *vast sensory information* as they reach out and touch the world. And they are tightly linked to language.

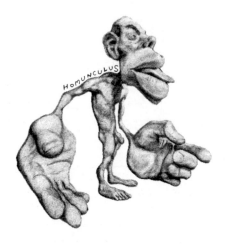

Intuitively it makes sense, since our hands *spoke* before we learned words. Research studies have demonstrated that when the hands move freely it enhances *word recognition*. For actors, how helpful to know this! No doubt another reason simple activities produce ease in memorization is because the *hands are free to move* around.

(I smiled recently when I read an interview with Christopher Walken – superb actor – where he said he learns his lines while cooking, with his script sitting on a music stand nearby.) Being active while learning lines is like a magic potion for many actors. Your anxiety level lowers. Your brain releases needed neurotransmitters, and you prepare a lovely dinner. Just think of all the time you have spent trying to learn lines lying in bed, wondering why it's so hard.

Memorization strategies: You are rewiring your brain!

Now that you know you can get your neurotransmitters flowing, let's quickly talk about some memorization strategies. Almost every actor will tell you that if a director gives specific blocking, those movements, repeated in rehearsals, help lock in lines – there's that *physical connection* again. 'I talk about the gun when I am at the desk', etc. I urge you to really utilize those physical cues by drilling the lines at home after each rehearsal, while trying to do the blocking. If you have not been given specific blocking, your moving around to make your bed, cook dinner or get dressed will at least connect your body to the text.

Always speak aloud. Don't mumble. Really say the words. This doesn't mean saying them *lovingly, oozing with meaning*. You need to speak the words in a full voice so that several senses can be operating simultaneously. Your *ears will be hearing* the words, the *muscles of your mouth and throat* will be producing the sounds and *your eyes* will be moving between your physical task and the script, actually printing a picture of those words as they sit on the page. *The more alive your senses, the better for your memory as your senses are actually triggers for memory and the firing of the neurons.*

Repetition, saying those words over and over and over is unfortunately the key. The good news is the way the brain is wired and how incredibly 'plastic' it is throughout our lives. We are literally able to create more brain space for this skill, the more frequently we do it. This means you will begin to memorize faster and faster – repeating the lines sometimes only a few times before they are lodged into your deep memory storage. This kind of drilling *is essential* for the neurochemical reaction you want. I admit this is the least 'sexy' part of acting.

An actor I was directing in a play complained that a very long speech she had was simply not 'sticking' no matter how hard she tried. I suggested she go home that night and repeat it seventy-three times – actually making a note each time. The next day the speech was effortless. Knowing I had playfully suggested that number, with a smile she said it was actually word-perfect by the twenty-eighth time. There's no substitute for that kind of repetition.

There is a technique that musicians use when learning music that is equally helpful for actors. It is called 'gathering'. And, just as the musician is not deeply concerned with phrasing or dynamics when learning the notes, you don't need to focus on meaning or acting. You are only trying to lock the picture and sound of those written words into your neurons. Gathering works like this: you speak aloud a phrase or sentence – and please don't forget to move around. 'To be or not to be, that is the question.' When you are *sure* you can say this several times without looking at the text you move on to the next phrase. When that is secure you go back to the first and put the two together and so forth, always going back to the beginning.

With a monologue you will probably *do this in chunks*, learning *seven* lines well, before moving on to the next seven and then putting the two chunks together. In the end you will have spoken those words many, many times. Actors generally want to rush this process and so become satisfied with *almost knowing*. *Almost* is not good enough. The brain then uses only 'short-term storage', which is not dependable. You need to push the words into 'long-term storage' so they are automatic. The acid test is to see if you can repeat the monologue at *lightning speed while taking a shower*. If you need to pause to think of the next word or phrase, it is not securely learned.

I understand if this sounds arduous. It is *at first*. You are creating patterns in your brain. There is a saying now in neuroscience, **'neurons that fire together, wire together'**. You are promoting this wiring every time you memorize in this way. That also means that it will get *easier and easier*. Your brain will develop the pattern for this unique memorizing behaviour. It's almost as though you create a channel in your brain that gets deeper and more efficient the more you use it – like building muscles when you work out.

Because the brain retains a great deal of plasticity – the ability to keep adapting – throughout our lives, the more you repeat these techniques the more deeply embedded they will become in your brain. Most important of all: *do not forget the motor cortex connection to memory and emotion*. Think how energized you can be folding laundry while learning a piece you've loved for years. Cleaning your flat, great! Working out, yes!

In every class that I teach I challenge the actors to memorize a new monologue every week. And I mean it. Those who take up the challenge tell me how amazed they are. Within six months they are memorizing at a speed and ease they could not have imagined. We are all capable of being 'quick studies'. If you wonder how the actors in Shakespeare's company learned so many plays, you can read the recently published book, *Shakespeare's Education* by Kate Emery Pogue. She describes the prodigious amount of memorization throughout the education of the period. Their brains were well trained. No wonder they were so good at it.

An invaluable skill for auditions

The ability to memorize quickly has very practical application. Think about those television auditions where you arrive at the sign-in desk and they hand you a few pages of script. The receptionist says, 'You aren't expected to memorize this, just get comfortable with it so we can put you on camera.' **From now on you will smile as you head for the nearest stairwell or out onto the street where you can move around.** Going up and down stairs is great. Unlike the other actors in the waiting room who are trying to figure out how to 'act' this script, you will get your neurotransmitters surging. The lines will sink in like lightning. You can look toward the camera with confidence. You will connect to your Dungeon and be fully 'alive' for your audition. By the way, even if you have learned the lines thoroughly, hold the script in one hand. Then even if you don't happen to need to look at it, you have it there just in case.

One of the *biggest gifts you can give yourself is your ability to learn an audition script quickly.*

The ball is now in your court

It's time for you to get to work, trying out this new approach. Your first assignment is to learn some of the very short pieces below. **Don't try to act them or figure them out!** *Just learn the words.* You will be using these in our work together when we go through *self-tuning. But don't panic.* If you want to use the *audio link* for the emotional work in the next chapter, I will be prompting you – speaking each line of these short pieces *for you to repeat after me*. That means *you don't have to memorize them now.* You see I understand that you are probably itching to experience the emotional connection to those words.

Please do try learning a *new monologue or poem* that appeals to you to *practise memorizing in this new way.* You cannot practise this skill too much. We are moving into accessing your emotions and *you will want solidly memorized text to explore and savour those feelings.*

A very important warning. **As you first read through these short pieces, please resist the temptation to figure how they relate to you; to whom you might be speaking.** All those Freudian connections that seem so interesting won't be helpful. *These are just words attached to feelings that live inside you.* Our goal is to *turn off the Intellect!* Try not to whinge too much learning these 'poems' or a new monologue. **Think how many tedious chores you can do at the same time!**

EXERCISES

Very short pieces to connect to your Dungeon

Come here
Please, come here.
I need you.
I try so hard to please you.
I do everything for you.
I wanted to make you happy.
I love you.
You never see me.
You never see anything.
Please.
I need you.

Stay with me
Stay with me.
I'm frightened.

Please don't leave me.
I'll be all alone.
Please.
I'll have no one.
Don't go.
Take me with you.
I need you.
Please, don't leave me.

I waited
I waited.
I didn't make a sound.
I had no one.
I had no one to protect me.
I was all alone.

I was too little.
Where were you?
It hurt.
I needed you.
I needed you to protect me.
Where were you?

Never good enough
I always have to work so hard.
Why do you make it so hard?
It's never good enough.
I always do it wrong
Please don't be angry.
I need you to help me.
You frighten me.
Please.
I'm doing my best.
Please, I love you.

**Why are you always
angry?**
Why?
I hate it.
It frightens me.
I need you to help me.
Please don't yell at me.
I love you.
Hold me.
Hold me in your arms.
Tell me that you love me.
Just, please, don't be angry.

I try so hard
Please, don't be angry

I need you.
I try so hard to please you.
I do everything for you.
I wanted to make you happy.
I love you.
You never see me.
Don't go.
Please.
Why can't you love me?

Stay with me
Please stay with me.
I'm frightened.
Please don't leave me.
I'll be all alone.
Please.
I'll have no one.
Don't go.
Take me with you.
I need you.
I need you to stay with me.
Don't leave me.
I'll die.

I waited
I waited for you.
I didn't make a sound.
I had no one.
I had no one to protect me.
I was all alone.
I was too little.
Where were you?
It hurt.
I needed you.

I needed you to protect me.
It wasn't my fault.
Where were you?

Never good enough
I always have to work so
    hard.
Why do you make it so hard?
It's never good enough.
I always do it wrong.
What's wrong with me?
Please don't be angry.
I need you to help me.
I can't do it alone.
You frighten me.
Please.
I'm doing my best.
Please, I love you.

**Why can't you help
me?**
You are always angry.
Why?
I hate it.
It frightens me.
I need you to help me.
It's too hard for me to do
    alone.
Please don't yell at me.
I love you.
Hold me.
Hold me in your arms.
Tell me that you love me.
Just don't be angry.

Stop hurting me!
Stop hurting me!
You always hurt me.
I hate it.
You don't know me at all.
You taught me to hate you.
Leave me alone.
I hope you never come back.
I loved you.
I will never love you again.
I will never forgive you.
I loved you so much.

I needed you
I needed you to protect me.
I couldn't protect myself.
I was too little.
It wasn't my fault.
It was your fault.
I will never forgive you.
Never!
I will hate you forever.
I was so afraid.
I could have died.
I hope you die.
I needed you.
No more guilt!

Don't touch me!
You are standing too close.
I can't breathe.
I hate it.
Get away.
Get away from me!

Don't touch me.
I hate you.
Keep your hands off me.
You make me sick.
You touch me and I will kill
    you.

I hope you die
I hate your anger.
I hate it.
You don't know anything.
You don't know me at all.
You're the stupid one.
You never saw me, ever!
I hope you die.
I loved you so much.
I did everything for you.
I hope you never come back.

Get away from me!
Leave me alone.
Get away from me.
And don't touch me.
Get your fucking hands off me!
You hurt me so much.
I wanted to die.
You made me hate you.
You touch me and I will kill
    you.
I will fucking watch you die.

I will love it.
I will win!

I want you to see me!
Look at me.
You never see me.
I want you to see how much you
    hurt me.
I want you to see how much I
    loved you.
I can't carry you around any
    more.
I'm sorry.
I love you, but I will never forgive
    you.
Look at me.
I'm not a transportation system!
It's my life!

It's my turn
It's my turn to fight back.
It's my turn to stop you.
It's my turn to be strong.
It's my turn to be protected.
It's my turn to be held in your
    arms.
It's my turn to be loved.
It's my turn to be happy.
You can't stop me.
It's my turn to win!

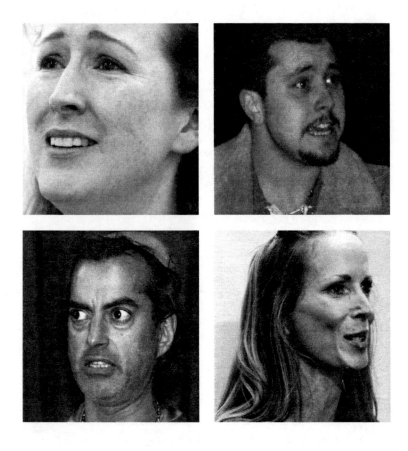

3

A CONVERSATION WITH YOUR INTELLECT AND DUNGEON: BEFORE WE *TUNE*

The first day of one of my *acting with passion* workshops, an actor who had waited to volunteer until the very last, said, 'This is all very interesting. But it's not going to work for me. I had a perfect childhood. I don't think I had any pain or fear. I was always encouraged, protected and adored.' I answered that I thought that was great and that we would see what his body had or did not have stored in the muscles.

He stood in front of the class. *I touched his chest with the palm of my hand and he burst into heaving sobs.* In fact he discovered huge feelings inside himself and became quite a fan of the work, attending many workshops. Each time he would shake his head and say, 'I have no idea where any of that comes from.'

One of the most exciting facts is that most of us don't know *where a great deal of our complex emotional machinery comes from*. I believe it is *an irrelevant question*. We don't need to know. All we need is to trust that it is all there. In fact, I'm convinced we, human beings, sharing identical limbic systems, possess all of the *same core feelings*: love, betrayal, fear, rage, loss, greed, joy – just to name a few. Isn't it obvious when you think about it? Else how could we understand plays written over 2,000 years ago? Coming from cultures other than our own? Plays about experiences vastly different than our own? How many of us have had our father poisoned by our uncle and a ghost appears to tell us about it? Yet those core emotions of abandonment, betrayal, vengeance, love, resonate in all of us.

The human journey inevitably is filled with an enormous range of feelings. As you explore yours you will find emotions bubbling up that are full and true and yet have *no logical connection to events in your life*. This work is simply not *memory based* in any way. Let me repeat that.

Acting with passion does not draw on any conscious memories. That's fortunate for actors because memory is quite a complex brain process. Freud had hoped that by 'free association' we could pull whole memories from both our conscious and unconscious minds. This has proved to be far from the case. Remembering the 'stories' of our lives is *elaborate and not very accurate*. Neuroscientists tell us that we hold memories in a *series of still photos*, often with gaps of seconds or minutes or longer in between. When we tell someone about that birthday party long ago, as we are telling the remembrance, we are *filling in those gaps* to make the story complete. Each time we repeat that story we continue to edit and change it slightly. Our brain seems to store each latest version. Terribly curious, isn't it? *And all of us thought we could just call up the film of that birthday and see it accurately*.

You have noticed that I talk about the unconscious and conscious mind. These are labels that science has created to try to understand one of our greatest mysteries.

What is our unconscious mind?

It is the world of our dreams and unpredictable emotional outbursts that can be so frightening. For an actor, it is your playground. What is interesting is that **neuroscience has been unable, at this time, to *locate* this playground**. Neuroscientists can show you where in the brain you see straight lines, and where you see curved lines. Where you see colours. Where you hear rhythm and where you hear melody. But they have no idea where the unconscious can actually be found.

At the beginning of each workshop I talk to actors about owning feelings in their bodies. As I describe body armour and how *emotions are locked away in muscular tension*, I notice ripples of feelings on the actors' faces as they take in this concept. Their eyes sometimes mist. Their cheeks tremble ever so slightly. It is as though the Intellect has become so interested in the *dangerous* things I'm talking about that it has slipped away from guarding the Dungeon door to listen better. And . . . *then the door is able to crack open.* Light filters in. The emotions in the Dungeon are listening actively to what I am saying. I imagine them looking up at the opening door saying, 'We're going to get out!'

I am evidently speaking to the actors' unconscious minds, *as I hope I am speaking to yours.* Oops, before your Intellect says, 'Hang on a minute,' I'll acknowledge that the Intellect is listening like mad.

Understanding your Intellect

When you were little, trying to make sense of your complicated world, **part of your *conscious mind*** was busy *trying to figure things out for you, to help you and keep you safe.* 'Oh, that taller big person with the scratchy face, who seems to be very important to the softer big person who gives me milk to drink, is called Dad.'

Even as I quote those realizations, none of them, in those first two years, are within access of conscious memory. We think we remember things when we hear stories about what we did or said at age one. We know how suggestible the mind is. (There's been a raging controversy over the planting of 'false memory' by therapists – if you wish to know more!) Instead, the Intellect (*one facet* of your conscious mind) is developing its repertoire of *advice* and the unconscious – tightly connected to the limbic system – is absorbing the messages of danger storing those away as well.

As you get older, your conscious mind is still learning masses of information – all the learning you will be using throughout your life. *This is now being stored into memories you can access.* 'Two plus two equals four.' Meanwhile, that other part of your conscious mind does its best to help you figure out many confusing things – *why sometimes those two adults, Mum and Dad, are happy with you and why, for no reason you can explain, they are not so happy.* **Thus, the part of your conscious mind assigned to understanding these dynamics and *protecting you* from their dangers seems to grow a separate identity.** I have called it the Intellect.

Your Intellect was trying to protect you, to anticipate problems for you, to make sense of bizarre situations. *Why did those parents seem angry with you* when that awful, loud-speaking person called Mrs Smith nearly smothered you because she gripped you so tightly it hurt and you howled to be rescued? Why did they bring that *new* tiny baby into the house when *you* were their *darling* baby?

Remember, we are talking about a *very young conscious mind doing its best*. How distressing and confusing the world becomes when the adults who had been nurturing – who snared you into their contract of loving them in exchange for your survival – suddenly change the rules. Overnight, it seems, you must stop screaming when you want something. You have to *use words* – still a shaky matter. You are punished if you get angry, when anger seems like the only *logical* response. And, heaven forbid you should harm that new baby who screams whenever *it* wants to and is never reprimanded.

Little by little your Intellect constructs logic around these events and begins advising you. 'Be careful, don't make Daddy angry or something bad will happen.' 'Don't cry. Smile, that pleases Mummy.' It gives you rules to follow: *Only bad little girls show their anger. Cry-babies are stupid. Being brave and strong is good.*

As you get older, your Intellect continues to interpret the world around you. *But at some point in your childhood it seems to get stuck.* **As you grow up it continues to look at everything through assumptions made during those early formative years.** The voice in your head sounds like it is growing up, but the *perceptions are terribly inaccurate.*

As a therapist I treated a man who told me he was terrified to talk to his father who was 'enormous, strong and intimidating'. A former US Marine, his dad did sound pretty scary. I suggested he invite his father to a session, as generalized fear was a huge issue for my patient. In walked a slightly stooped older man with a hesitant manner.

The father who once barked orders and punished savagely *no longer existed*. My patient was now actually quite a bit taller than his father. This fact came as a *surprise* to him when I pointed it out. He had *retained an image* captured when he was probably no more than seven – when his father's temper and power had been terrifying. As you explore your irrational feelings you will begin to experience the realization that the people *you* once feared are now 'ghosts' – they no longer exist.

Many irrational fears, rules that seem to apply only to you, limitations others can't see, are usually the distortions coming from your Intellect's young perceptions.

You are an actor. You want to play Medea – a character who has no problem whatsoever in showing her anger. You begin a speech describing the injustice you've suffered and your desire for revenge. Suddenly you feel your body tense. Your throat constricts. The emotions you *understand clearly* in the text don't seem to stir. The voice in your head says, 'You need to be angry. You need more emotion.' So you scream louder and only end up hurting your throat – the screams seem empty.

Because at the same time your Intellect is trying to 'direct you' and tell you how Medea should be acted, *at the exact same time* it is guarding your Dungeon to make sure that no *real* anger gets out.

The reason for this is not that your Intellect wants you to fail, but it is operating from those child assumptions. 'If you show anger something terrible will happen! Anger is bad. It is dangerous! You must get it under control and be a good little girl!'

There in a nutshell you have the dilemma of the power of your Intellect in suppressing the emotional impulses that live in your unconscious. It stands guard over your Dungeon so that *even while it is 'directing' you to express this or that emotion*, it is making sure it will be impossible.

'The slings and arrows of outrageous fortune' do not end at the age of three

Although I believe certainly that much of who we are and the armour we've built was created in the first years of our lives, *beyond memory*, realistically we certainly didn't freeze our personalities at age three. We continued to be formed by many influences: Our families most certainly, but also friends, neighbours, society, events beyond anyone's control.

The pool of memories an acting teacher might have asked you to search through to find relevance with a role or situation cannot be written off as inconsequential. You have a vast array of memories – many have had a profound impact on you. Your armour, your interactions with the world, continued to be shaped as you grew older, as you encountered bullying classmates, sadistic teachers, family upheavals, rejecting lovers. So, in light of our mind-body approach to acting, how do we treat those experiences and memories? *I believe those experiences continued and still continue to impact our armour, adding more layers to our muscular tension.* Chronic back pain is often the result. Present-day events link up and join others already in your Dungeon so that when you act you will experience a jumble of feelings, not specific memories.

The fortress

I've been describing body *armour*, using Reich's term. However, in reality, when I look at some actors' bodies and touch their muscles I feel I am encountering a fully constructed fortress. There are many different styles – some are made of brick and cement, others seem to be made out of Plexiglas. The Plexiglas model is familiar to actors who feel as though there is some kind of invisible wall between them and the world. They realize they never really *see* the eyes and faces of others with the clarity they know they should. They've been given bewildering criticism from acting teachers for this. Some actors' fortresses give the appearance they are peering out at us through narrow arrow slits. Within every fortress, I see the frightened child cowering inside, hoping this fortification will keep the danger out.

For some children, life at home *felt* like a war zone. The actor might recall volatile, painful scenes. His body holds terror. He has experienced enough fear and danger in childhood to militarize his body with muscular tensions in preparation for an attack. Building that fortress might have meant survival.

Almost all homes feel like a war zone to a child from time to time. Mum is stressed because she isn't sleeping since the new baby came. Dad hates his job. The plumber didn't arrive and the water has been turned off in half the house. You are terribly curious and couldn't help it that you reached up high and broke a precious antique vase. Need I go on?

Having raised four children myself – two wonderful children of my own and two wonderful step-children – I can testify *personally* that **parents do not wake up each morning saying to themselves,**

'I wonder how I can make my child crazy today?' We do it *without effort* because parenting isn't an easy job. Also, don't forget, your parents had parents.

The important thing for you to understand is that if you feel as though you go through life carrying your need for protection, *body tight, on high alert*, you can look forward to the *challenges and joys of dismantling that muscular effort*. A dead giveaway is how you feel at the end of a long day – exhausted by carrying around a fortress? *Being vigilant every moment*, waiting for the blow to strike, makes every day difficult and acting painfully hard. Being told to relax only makes you feel that you must be crazy.

How complicated we are! 'I love you!' and 'I hate you!' are both true

At the same time an actor and I explore the terror locked in the muscles of her body, and we unlock the anger and pain connected to it, we always discover an amazing amount of love. *Children are full of love*. We come into the world instinctively needing to bond with a caregiver and very quickly this need morphs into love. How complicated the human journey that the very people with whom we are *most deeply enraged* are also the people we have loved and needed the most.

Here you are, a little savage, just beginning to learn the rules. Great Aunt Betty has come to visit. Mum and Dad want you to shine. Instead you howl and kick when she tries to pick you up. 'Be sweet, darling. We love Aunt Betty. Say you are sorry.' You are only two and a half and answer, 'She smells funny.' *War zone alert!* You see looks of anger and rejection on your parents' faces. 'Go to your room and don't come out until you can be nice. You are a bad little girl.' Because you are confused and hurt, your immediate protective emotion (this is instinct, remember) is fury. You stamp your foot as you flee to your room. Dad shouts, 'Don't you dare stamp your foot again, or you will be punished.'

Enter, guilt. When a child is disciplined it feels angry because of this withdrawal of love – at that moment the parents are focused on *fixing the behaviour* and probably dealing with their own demons momentarily (failing as a parent in front of Aunt Betty). The anger, and even horror, a child sees on the adult face is translated into, 'I must be a very, very bad person. They can't love me any more.' Guilt.

This thought clicks into several survival fears: 'without these adults to love and protect me, I will die.' We're into fight or flight. Since you *can't escape, fight* is what surfaces. Rage (with its surges of adrenaline and epinephrine) is the emotion that enables us to fight for our survival. Unfortunately, when you are very young this generally translates into a tantrum combining the rage with your *powerlessness and fear.*

When you were very young these *tantrums could feel as though you were in danger of bursting apart.* We know from observation that the child loses control physically, falling on the floor, kicking, unable to stop the screaming and sobbing. Quite often in working with an actor, where we will begin to release rage, simultaneously alarm bells go off. The body begins to clamp down in terror. I believe that's because the body is receiving messages that say, 'release of these feelings means you will completely fall apart and trigger unforgivable behaviours'.

We also know from later adult recollections that these tantrums were much more destructive to the child than to the parents. Long after the tantrum is over the child carries *a buried fear that an evil, dangerous force lives inside them.* The child determines to *hide* this at all costs. The actor faced with a role like Coriolanus or Electra would have to go to extraordinary lengths to produce the anger necessary when the Intellect has *classified that anger as dangerous and pushed those feelings into the muscles of the body creating chronic tensions.* Actors feel themselves churning and pushing *manufactured feelings* instead of releasing *real* ones.

Looking at the instinctive cycle: rejection/fear of abandonment/ fight or flight/rage, we see deeply embedded primal survival instincts. As any anthropologist will tell you, *this encompasses the instinct to kill when attacked.* 'You threaten my survival, I will defend myself to the death.' **Thus we see at the tender age of around two and a half, that the human animal first experiences killer rage** – *the urge to commit murder.*

Parents are aghast when their two-year-old begins waking in the middle of the night screaming from nightmares – typical at this age. The parent thinks, 'How is that possible? I've never let my child watch a frightening TV programme. I don't read scary stories to him. Why is he saying monsters are trying to hurt us all?' The terrifying monster is the rage that has blossomed inside – *a confusing rage because it is crying out for the destruction of the very people the child loves the most.*

The saddest outcome of this instinctive process is that the guilt after these rages is horrible. It then feeds a new scenario. 'I have this ugly, gnarly thing inside me. It is fearful and destructive. If anyone ever saw it or knew about it, they would not be able to love me.' We carry this *dark secret*, thinking we are *alone in this guilt*. You can imagine the laughter that erupts in a class when everyone discovers *we all share the same secret!*

How wonderful for an actor to realize that the convoluted *efforts of acting the desire to kill are unnecessary*. All an actor needs to do is connect to those young feelings and wow! Savage, vicious, murderous feelings are available with ease. Just think how much of theatre is caught in this human dilemma – how many plays deal with the complexity of I love you and I hate you both being true. Isn't the dysfunctional family a pretty popular theme?

At first, when you begin to ease the muscular armour that holds back anger, don't be alarmed if you experience a natural internal conflict. Even as you, the actor, *want to release the feelings*, your internal monitor (the Intellect) will be fighting to hide them. This is normal and part of the process. On the positive side for you, lucky actors, is that *having murderous rage and love/hate inside you means you can play all the roles that once seemed beyond your grasp*. Think of the frustrations in trying to 'relate' to many different characters through your *own* autobiography. None of us, I hope, can draw upon having murdered anyone in reality. Ah, but at two and half, we certainly did plenty of that in our minds.

So many things to be guilty about

A little girl runs, falls down and scrapes her knee. She comes howling to the grown-ups. She is showered with hugs and kisses. 'Ouch. Hurtie-hurt.' (Cuddle, cuddle, kiss, kiss.) A little boy runs, falls down and scrapes his knee. He comes howling to the grown-ups. He's given a sharp pat on the back. 'No crying. Be a brave little soldier. There. Doesn't hurt, does it?' *There are exactly the same number of nerve endings in a little boy's knee as there are in a little girl's.* The message to 'be a man' is one of the most powerful in almost every culture.

We often find ourselves laughing in my classes as we explore the absurdity of the phrase, 'Be a Man!' It is especially *ludicrous* when we think of how often this instruction is given to *little boys*. What could be more impossible? Yet the guilt encountered around this nonsensical command is incredible. How many grown men carry around a terrible shame for the *terrible crime* of not being a full-grown, six-foot tall, powerful man by the age of seven?

I've worked with actors who have obviously spent long hours working out to develop huge muscles – broad chests, bulging biceps. All testifying to the fact that 'Now I am strong.' Underneath this *warrior exterior* is the terrified child, *never strong enough*. Of course, no amount of body-building can assuage the guilt of once being powerless and *not being able to fight back*.

Now lest you think that little boys cornered the market on bravery and guilt, I have worked with women whose bravery as children was clearly heroic. I urge *everyone* to say one of my favourite phrases – one I hope you will speak with pleasure when you learn to *tune* yourself: ***NO MORE GUILT!***

You've noticed that I am speaking of all of these 'psychological issues' from a completely personal voice. They are an amalgam of my personal journey as therapist, actor, director, passionate learner of neuroscience, parent and fellow frightened child. There are few definitive answers in the psychology world. The more you learn the more counter-arguments you hear. Much of this is theory and subjective. I am sharing *my take* on all this complexity and how it affects actors. And I am fearfully opinionated sometimes.

These are the realizations from my years of teaching *acting with passion*. For example, I've been deeply touched to see how often I find in actors such strong *urges to take care of others*, always making sure everyone is alright. I see in their bodies children who have taken on an adult role far too young. These *little adults* are often asked to take responsibility for the happiness of one or even both parents, or be an adjunct parent to siblings. In class I describe how children learn to *carry around whole families* on their backs. Once you start carrying one person around, others seem eager to join them. The actor as an adult continues to unconsciously accept this role – his body now accustomed to being weighed down. 'Okay, everybody, climb aboard.' Many actors, hearing this, nod in recognition. One of our *self-tuning* phrases is: **'I can't carry you around any more. I'm not a transportation system.'**

Whatever 'role' you learned to play in your family, the frustration, of course, is when you become an actor and *wish to go beyond this role*. You might understand this in terms of the 'limitations' others suggest you have. Agents or casting directors will be quick to tell you that you aren't 'right' for a certain part. Yet you know deep down that you can do the role. Actors come to me terribly frustrated that they are only sent up for a very narrow range of roles, their agent convinced that they can't play anything else.

Your agent is responding to your 'act' and to your armour. If you've learned to negotiate your way through being pleasant, agreeable and self-effacing, *you have learned how to communicate these personality traits so effectively* that they shine through even when you don't want them. If you say to your agent, 'Please send me up for Hedda Gabler,' your agent will look at you like you're crazy.

If you've perfected hiding any vulnerability so you could appear to be strong and ready for a fight, it will be hard to convince the casting director you can do Tusenbach. As you explore releasing your armour and you begin to express feelings that are outside of your usual 'role', you will find these artificial limitations on your range will disappear. *When you begin to utilize the full, complicated variety of your feelings*, you may feel little urges of resistance now and then or even a reminder that 'This could be dangerous.' **In truth, the most dangerous thing that could happen is that you might receive a BAFTA or Academy Award!**

4
SELF-TUNING: THE KEYS TO THE KINGDOM

Fortunately, the connections between *your body and your brain* are even more powerful than the voice of the frightened child that lives in your head. We must harness that power so you can count on it every time you act.

In a few minutes you're going to put down the book and begin your first exploration of *self-tuning*. For example, you will *touch your face*, as we know the tiny muscles lurking there have spent years reminding you to hide feelings. Think of how often you've seen fellow actors looking like they are wearing a kind of mask. They stand up to act and their face is not the same as it was ten minutes earlier during the break when you were all talking together. You've probably felt it in yourself at times. *Children learn to construct a mask very early*. They are trying to please those adults and know that revealing various emotions will not be well received. A popular parental command is, 'Wipe that expression off your face.' Interesting, hmm?

We begin with your face and upper body since this is the armour that tends to be the most obvious and hence easiest for us to approach, and then move on to the whole body. Think about what actors we all became at a very early age.

- We learned to make a neutral face, not permitting the muscles around the mouth and eyes to express anger. We lifted the chin and made 'brave shoulders' that didn't reveal how frightened we really were.

- We learned to smile when we were sad, even as the chest began to tighten and we wanted to cry.

- We developed muscles under our eyes to prevent tears, and tension in the neck to control the back of the throat where crying really begins.

- We learned to clench our jaw and tighten our lips to suppress disagreeable sounds or words – even as the stomach would clench, knees begin to lock and hands become rigid.

- We became expert at tightening all the muscles that move the pelvis so that any expression of anger would be immediately suppressed – often a smile might be produced at the same time.

- The mask, securely in place, fooled everyone, no matter how heavy and tight the armour became.

These habits produced masks and armour that protected us – or so it seemed at the time. The problem for actors is that *with the tiniest 'danger' cue, all those muscle groups are recruited*. Hardly helpful for an on-camera audition!

Of course the insidious facts about these tensions is that they are triggered by your Intellect and also *deep in your unconscious – in your limbic system where your survival instincts have been threatened*. Trying to 'relax' the muscles as in a classic 'relaxation' process would do you no good. Nor do you have the luxury of a half-hour relaxation at the moment you are cued that the camera is rolling.

Instead, we are going to signal directly to the muscles with movement and touch. Do not underestimate the remarkable *sensory feedback from the lightest touch*. We are so accustomed to forcing our bodies to do difficult things. 'Lift that leg higher, pull up your knees!' shouts the ballet master. 'Add another twenty push-ups and add another mile to your morning run.' Doesn't that sound good?

Acting with passion will take you down a different road. You can work out as vigorously as you wish. But to *tune* yourself and access your emotions on cue takes a more nurturing, gentle approach. Let's take a moment and marvel at the sensitivity your skin. Yes, that outer layer we carry around and never think about unless it itches. **Your skin is one your most potent sense organs.** Doctors frequently note the connection between emotions and the skin. You will learn to communicate with this fragile bundle of sensitivity with the lightest of touches. As you feel this touch reverberate throughout your body you will learn to trust the powerful messages you can send with so little effort.

Opening the Dungeon activates the *entire* body and *all* of your feelings. Even though Reich attributed specific feelings to specific areas of the body, *I have found them to be quite intertwined*. In your Dungeon, they all live together: joy, surprise, hate, love, anger, fear, greed, abandonment and infinitely more. *Don't be surprised if you encounter anger when you open your broken heart or touch sadness, only to then discover terror.*

Unlocking feelings through the release of these subtle tensions is like peeling an onion one little layer at a time. You may feel as though you have Mt Vesuvius living inside you, but we won't release it all at once. *So, patience please.* All we are looking for is a *crack* of the Dungeon door opening.

If you can work with a partner or a small group there are some advantages. *It is very helpful to see the muscular structures in someone else.* Looking in the mirror will not be particularly useful except now and then to check something specific. Ultimately however, **when you act you will be on your own** so learning to sense when your back is straight, your chest open and your arms free is your ultimate goal. If it is most likely you will be working through these exercises by yourself, you will be fine.

'Talking to your armour' by finding healthy alignment
[https://vimeo.com/102846703]

Stand comfortably. I'd like you to stand in your habitual way – note where your hands and arms want to be. Notice if you feel awkward or stiff when you take a moment to observe yourself. Notice your breathing. You can look in a mirror or ask for feedback from any actors doing this work with you. I want you to have a sense of how you stand when you aren't 'doing anything'.

Terrific! With the awareness of your *natural posture* in mind, please look at the illustration of a skeleton. We can learn a lot about our bodies from taking a peek into how our bones are structured.

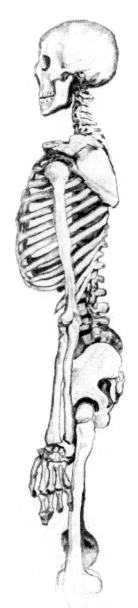

SKELETON

- Observe the journey of the spine from deep within your skull. Notice the three heavy structures the spine must support: your head, your shoulders and rib cage, and your pelvis.

- You'll notice that your head needs to float directly up in order not to strain the precarious balance on the narrow cervical (neck) vertebrae.

- You can see that the insertion of your arm bones into the shoulders leads the arms to hang directly at your sides, not resting towards the front of the body.

- You see how well protected the upper spine is by the heavy bones of the rib cage (housing your lungs, heart and other vital organs).

- You can see how well protected the lower vertebrae of the sacrum are with the strong pelvic bones.

- You can see the 'natural curves of the spine' quite easily.

- You can also see *how vulnerable the lower back* (below the ribs and above the bones of your pelvis) *and neck are to strain*, when you observe that there are no bony structures protecting them, *only muscles*.

With your skeleton in mind we will now begin adjusting your 'habitual' (if necessary) alignment into a healthier, natural alignment. Look down at your feet. You want them to be about outer-hip width apart and parallel, not turned out (duck footed) or turned in (pigeon toed.) You can roll around on your feet to make sure your weight isn't falling into your arches, or on the outside of your foot. Either one will cause a knock-on effect up to your knees, your thighs and into your pelvis.

Next, stand against a wall so you can get to know that spine a little better. Place your feet around six to eight inches (fifteen to twenty centimetres) away from the wall so you can rest your entire back against it. Let your muscles receive the feedback of simply *sensing that the wall is now helping you to stand up straight*.

(If leaning against the wall causes tension, step away and shake your body out before going back. Or abandon the wall altogether. You can do everything standing in the middle of the room and *imagining* the wall behind you.)

You may sense several things immediately.

- Is your chin up high with your head thrust back in order to make contact with the wall? *Tension in the neck and shoulders is almost universal.* The head is quite heavy for your narrow neck to carry around, *unless it's perfectly balanced.* Most of us also 'lead with the head' when we walk around in life. Our eyes are busy taking in the world so it's logical the head wants to jut forward. It's not, however, the way our skeleton was designed. Right now you are only checking to see *what your habitual pattern* is. Later, we'll talk about creating *new habits* for you body.

- Does it feel as though your entire shoulder and upper back can rest on the wall or just part of it? If not, don't force it, just breathe and be aware of what part of your upper back feels comfortably settled into the wall and where you feel it lifting away.

- What about along your whole back? Check out where it is touching the wall and where it has pulled away from it. Almost every kind of physical work, whether it's Pilates, yoga, Alexander or Feldenkrais, will talk about the *natural curves* of the spine. Leaning against the wall you have the best opportunity to explore these. *You would like your lower back not to press against the wall but follow its natural curve.*

- Experiment with *tucking your pelvis forward and then moving it back in a 'sway back'* position. If you thrust it back, you can create a large curve at your lower back. Thrusting it forward pushes that area into the wall. Explore this several times, gaining *awareness of your range of motion.* This should feel good. If it hurts your back, that means you are forcing. Be gentle.

- You want your pelvis right in the middle – the famous 'neutral pelvis' everyone talks about. Finally you will make the backward and forward movements of the pelvis smaller and smaller until you try to find the centre position. Your goal will be a perfectly balanced pelvis. We will be visiting this again and again as we explore this region of the body and all the feelings it holds. For now, you are just running a 'systems check'.

- Ideally you want a small curve in the spine just above where you can feel the back of your pelvis leaning against the wall – that's your lower back, *vulnerable to discomfort if it is tight*. The lower back should curve away from the wall with *just enough space for you to slip one hand into the curve*. If your hand is smashed when you reach back, then you know you are thrusting your pelvis too far forward. If there is a yawning gap above your hand, your pelvis is thrusting back.

Once you've settled the lower back it's time for us to carefully explore the muscles of the upper back, chest, neck, pelvis, legs and feet. We carry around a massive amount of *emotion* throughout the body. *A veritable treasure trove for the actor.*

A note to you: at any point you can move away from the wall and shake out your body or roll up and down your spine like a 'rag doll'. At first, figuring all this out, it is very easy to get tense in trying to do this perfectly. Remember, you can also do all of the next movements in the centre of the room if the wall inhibits you or causes tension.

Your body

- To wake up the shoulders, raise your arms to just below shoulder height, hands facing each other.

- Reach your hands forward as though you are trying to hand someone a present. Your shoulders will only go a few inches away from the wall, so don't force.

- Now, move them back and feel your shoulders settle against the wall. Do this back and forth movement three or four times, each time gathering the awareness of your *shoulder blades* pushing apart when they pull away from the wall and then settle into your back as you retreat. Soon you will have a sense of when the arms are 'in' the shoulder socket, where you want them.

- Now, let your arms hang at your sides and just make big circles with your shoulders, feeling your range of motion – and feeling the back of your upper arms and shoulders rubbing up and down against the wall. See if your shoulders can practically touch your ears and then see how far downward you can spiral them. Change direction. This should feel good. *We carry a lot of tension in those upper trapezius muscles!*

- **Crucial, not only to your alignment for health, but for your emotional freedom, are the muscles connecting your shoulders to your chest.** When you look at a human skeleton you see that the arm inserts into the shoulder socket to hang directly at the side of the body. Too many of us develop subtle tightness in the chest that teaches the arms to hang slightly forward with the hands falling on the thighs. This pulls the head of the shoulder forward. These are the muscles responsible for 'hunching' your back. Hunched over posture is fine if you are going to play certain characters, but not the beautifully aligned body you want to keep your instrument in tune.

- To find that natural arm position, all you need to do is **rotate your entire arm outward from the shoulder**, raising your arms just beneath shoulder height. As you look down at your arm you want to *see your inner elbow and palm facing the ceiling*. You will also feel a movement in your shoulder girdle. Your shoulder blades (those little 'wings' called scapula) will feel as though they are digging slightly into your back. Yes! That's what you want to feel. Let those opened arms fall gently to your sides, still turned outwards. *Then just turn the lower half of the arm*, from below the elbow, so your hands can now face the sides of your body. *You should then have your arms directly at your sides, with your palms facing your outer hips, not the front of your thighs*.

- I am detailing this shoulder issue because it is crucial to how the world sees you. With the head of the shoulder forward and arms hanging in the front of the body, people (casting directors and agents) will see you as passive and fearful. With the arms at the correct alignment, you will give the impression of confidence and strength. Which would you prefer?

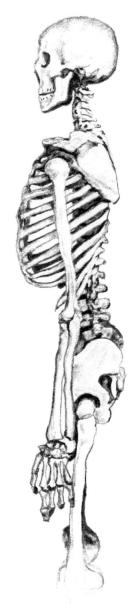

SKELETON

- Take stock. How does that feel? Can you sense that your chest is already far more open than usual?

- What are your eyes supposed to be doing? For most people, keeping your eyes closed for much of this will help you to really zone in on what your are feeling without distractions. (That's also why I think you'll find the audio prompts helpful.) If it bothers you to keep your eyes closed, let your gaze gently rest on the floor a few feet in front of you.

- If you are in a group and there's enough wall space, all of you can do this at the same time. You can also turn off the audio from time to time and chat about your heightened awareness for a few moments.

If you have found reworking your shoulder and arm position challenging, this might be an area you have strongly armoured – not unusual. This is one of those things you can check out in a mirror or ask your partner to look at. Let your arms and hands fall where they are most comfortable. If you see that the hands are facing with the palms inward and forward, touching the front of your thighs, you have just discovered a very helpful bit of information. Keep working at moving those shoulder blades into your back with your upper arm turning out. You have great fun in store as your body releases the old habit and embraces the new.

A final check on this area: place your arms in the 'stick 'em up' position. You would ideally like your entire arm at a right angle from the body, resting against the wall. While it is in this position – upper arm away from either side of the body, *bent elbow at shoulder height*, wrist, back of the hand – you are stretching muscles in your chest, back and shoulders. Don't panic if your arms and shoulders are unable to release enough so that your elbows can comfortably touch the wall. *You may also find it's just too hard right now to reach your hands that far back in this position*. That just tells us your shoulders are tight. Again, not unusual at all. This can now become your daily challenge. Try this every day for just a few minutes. Your goal is to let your back broaden, open and relax against the wall and your shoulders melt wide apart so that little by little those upper arms, elbows and hands can all rest on the wall in that 'stick 'em up shape'.

If you are experiencing a tightness in your lower back or the muscles in the area of your pelvis, it's a clear signal that we need to engage those muscles. Step away from the wall and try some pelvic thrusts, and circular movements with your hips. This should release some of that tension you may be feeling.

Time to take a quick break. Walk away from the wall, and with your knees slightly bent, just let your upper body fall forward like a rag doll. Roll your head a few times. Flutter your lips. Sigh. Shake out your arms and, with knees slightly bent, gently roll back up to standing. Wiggle around. You might want to take a drink of water before we get back to work. If you wish to review any of the alignment work, that's terrific. Just put me on 'pause' and I'll be waiting for you when you're ready to go through the next part of our *self-tuning*.

You'll see that we will go through this *tuning* together twice. The first time I'll be explaining things as we go, so that your conscious and unconscious minds can absorb the science behind the physical cues. The second time, I will talk you through each step and let your body and Dungeon absorb the experience. For now, just be sure you have some space around you to move comfortably.

Self-tuning with explanations

- Find your best alignment. Stand with your feet outer-hip distance apart. You want to feel very steady. Try to have your head well balanced and arms hanging at your sides.

- Pick up your left hand and glide your fingertips to touch the edge of your right shoulder, with your palm resting right where there is an indentation – where your shoulder inserts into the chest. *You are touching the muscles that hunch up your shoulders*. This position is familiar to most of us when we feel tired, discouraged or sad. As your hand glides into place, your gentle contact with skin or clothing along the path is sending messages to sensory receptors.

- You are touching very important muscles – those 'hunching muscles'. **I call them the Guardians of the Broken Heart.** Within your chest, where your heart lives, so much sadness and loss seems to collect. Not surprising that so many different languages have an expression equivalent to 'broken heart'. (Even though, anatomically, we now know the heart is just a pump and has nothing to do with feelings.)

- Your touch is speaking to all the muscles that learned to tense in response to sadness and loss. As children we think we must hide this sadness, either to protect the adults we love, or because we feel ashamed of it, or simply because it frightens us. We don't have to know 'why'. It's almost impossible, however, for *anyone to reach adulthood without a broken heart*. Along with this pain comes the body's response, which is to constrict the muscles of the chest in order to suppress the feelings. *That constriction becomes habitual*.

- As you rest your palm against those Guardians of the Broken Heart muscles you are speaking to those muscles. **That gentle pressure is saying, 'It's okay. We're okay.'**

- Now let that hand fall to your side and place the other hand on the opposite chest/shoulder connection. Just let it sit there, *the weight of the hand speaking to those muscles*. Don't try to rub or push. You want your muscles to respond to *gentle, subtle cues*. This gentle contact will begin to resonate, speaking to those muscles that have worked so hard to protect you.

- Next place one hand at the **centre of your chest** – women and men – at your breast bone. Feel the gentle pressure of your hand against your chest. **Breathe.** The skin and the many muscles that become tight when we are fearful or in pain, are all responding to the feeling of the weight and warmth of your hand. You are speaking directly to all the feelings in your chest. *Enjoy this moment of ownership of your complex sadness*.

- Next, place your other hand on the centre of your body, just above your navel. This is your upper stomach and the **musculature in front of the solar plexus** – a very sensitive part of the body – teeming with neurons. You can feel immediately that this very light pressure of the hand is communicating with the muscles that lie just beneath the skin. *You are saying hello to a lot of fear*.

- The solar plexus sits behind the upper region of the stomach and in front of the diaphragm. **Explore the feelings when your hand goes to your lower abdomen.** This is your digestive system and is rich in opiate receptors sensitive to fear. It contains countless radiating nerve fibres reaching almost every one of your vital organs. When you place your hand on either your upper or lower abdomen area *you are sending a message deep inside you to your primitive survival instincts*. One of the current theories is that we have a 'second brain' that dwells in the stomach, directly connected to the limbic system. This is where 'gut feeling' seems to come from and, for actors, entry to your Dungeon.

Your face and the 'windows of your soul'

- With one hand still resting on your solar plexus area, take your dominant hand and with your forefinger very gently, *light as a feather*, outline your mouth. **Gently brush the skin all around your mouth.** Don't rub or push. These are incredibly sensitive, *tiny* muscles. The slightest touch will wake them up. Enjoy the tingling you might feel – your skin is grateful for this reassuring touch. Your mouth has learned to *hide feelings*, to be brave, *to mask anger and hurt*. You are telling these muscles they don't have to be on alert 'to act'.

- Next take that finger and, again, light as a feather, **touch the skin beneath each of your eyes** – the windows of your soul. You are touching what I call the **bravery muscles**. They are the minute muscles just beneath the lower lid that have learned to hold back tears. How many of you have felt your eyes prickle with tears and yet none roll down your cheeks as you wish? It's your *bravery muscles* at work.

- You may feel a slight trembling in your face as you are doing this. Explore as you brush your cheek, your eyebrows, your forehead. The skin is one of our most dominant sensory organs – your light touch will set off trembling or tickling. That's terrific. *It's just your muscles waking up and coming to life*. By the way, that trembling looks terrific on camera.

- Please also stroke your eyebrows and those frown muscles in between. Amazing how much the *eyebrows want to help us act*, generally mimicking a child's effort to understand something too hard for them. If you've been told that you constantly move your eyebrows when you act, this gentle touch will say, 'you don't need to pretend to be grown up and wise'.

- **Now place a finger on your chin and tap it gently.** You are signalling your jaw to open. You want to teach your jaw to respond to this gentle tap rather that pushing or doing big jaw movements as one might in an aggressive voice warm-up. You want to keep opening your jaw and mouth with each tap until your mouth is wide open as if you could *take a bite out of a large apple*.

- Then breathe in – a lovely sharp intake of breath. **You will feel the back of the throat pop wide open.** Enjoy it. The muscles of the throat are very skilled at holding back sounds and feelings. *That's why actors have so many vocal problems*. The exact muscles we need to be pliant and relaxed have learned to tighten and constrict. *They were among the first muscles recruited when we all learned to hold back our screams and use words instead*. When the throat opens, we are reassuring all those muscles that the danger has passed.

- **Let a little voiced sigh escape with the next deep breath –** but please don't let it growl or try to use your lowest tones. You want to explore a *light, high, childlike sound*.

- **The child-like voice.** I will be asking you to find the voice most of you have worked very hard to put behind you. For boys reaching thirteen, fourteen or fifteen, those years when the vocal cords were thickening and your voice was changing were often a nightmare. Was there anything more humiliating than hearing yourself squeak? *How many actresses have worked to find the deep masculine tones* some acting teacher insisted on? For our purposes, *that gentle child voice must be encouraged and nurtured*. You will be using this to *tune* yourself because that voice is connected to your most hidden, illogical feelings. When you act, you will use your natural adult voice, of course – and those higher notes will resonate and strengthen your range.

Waking up your hands

- Your hands spoke before you did. They were one of your main messengers in interacting with the world. Not only did they grab and pull, **they actually began to communicate more directly by motioning to the adults**. They motioned their dislike when they would push things away. And they signalled clearly when they wanted something. As an infant your hands would make *little fists and then open with fingers extended*. This motion was repeated over and over again throughout your days as your *hands said, without words*, 'Come here!', 'Hold me!', 'Don't leave me!', 'I need you now!'

- As you grew older, you learned to talk and were daily forced to find alternatives to your most primitive means of expression. You learned to say, 'I understand', 'I'll wait my turn', 'I'm sorry'. You were told not to touch things, to 'keep your hands to yourself'. *Slowly, words and civilized behaviours became your new habits and your hands became polite.*

- This was another way we all learned to 'act'. We learned to hide our need for immediate attention and gratification and our hands stopped being our main means of communicating. *You are going to wake them up and ask them to 'speak for you' again.* My years of experience have shown me that **the muscles in your hands never forget**. They are just waiting for permission to be heard again. Hands are deeply connected to our needs. Our need for love, attention, safely, protection.

- Reach your hands out in front of you, arms around shoulder height, *palms facing each other*. You want your elbows almost straight but not locked, as though you are reaching for someone just beyond you. With your hands in this position, *look at them and ask your hands to make gentle fists, then release the fists, letting your fingers straighten – these are the reaching and grabbing motions your infant hands made.* **Try not to force this movement or make your hands 'dance'.** Gently, palms open, make a fist, then open again and repeat. Do this slowly several times. Your Intellect will try to instruct you to make this movement more 'interesting'. When infants do this, it is a simple straightforward set of movements: close hands, open hands and reach. *They seem to have no urge to do this with variety or drama.*

- You are attempting to **simulate the exact movements** you made with your hands before you spoke. As you do this, those movements will speak directly to your *unconscious* and the *emotions living in your Dungeon.*

- While reaching your hands out and motioning in this way I think it's *helpful to keep your eyes open*. Try to focus on your hands. **Just *see* them.** That's all. *You don't have to think any particular thoughts* because we are just stirring old feelings. **If you are in a group, look directly into their eyes.** *Do not try to visualize something* you think will urge feelings. That will be counterproductive, and put you in the grips of your Intellect.

- Your hands are actually speaking many words: 'Come here, don't leave me, I love you, please, I need you, I'm frightened.' You will recognize them from the short poems you learned. As you go further with your *self-tuning* and put all of this together you can feel free to say these words aloud in a gentle, child-like voice and sense how your hands and the words connect. *Don't try to figure out meaning or memory.* Just be curious.

- You might feel your chin rise when you first speak some of those phrases. This movement seems to be one of the earliest 'bravery' responses as it signals the throat to hold back crying. How often have you heard someone say, 'Chin up!', encouraging you to be brave?

- Actors *sometimes* see images relating to the spoken phrases, but most often not. When you are *really seeing* (rather than trying to visualize something), either your hands, or parts of the room, or your fellow actors' faces, you will find your Intellect retreating.

- Once again, there is a temptation to attach 'meaning' to the short poems. 'I wish I could have said that to my Dad. I remember the day when . . .' Your Intellect would like to *sabotage this process*, trying to take you right back to emotional recall and self-psychoanalysis. *The less meaning you attach* to these phrases the more directly they will connect to your Dungeon and your most exciting feelings.

Your lower body: Pelvis, hips, legs and feet

We are now moving into the emotions often seen as dangerous. We will explore the armour generally created to hold back *rage*. There's no doubt this is an emotional landscape that is much more frightening for most of us. (You might have been shocked, even horrified, by some of the phrases in the poems I asked you to memorize.) Just be assured, rage does not descend on us from nowhere. **It is *always* connected to *pain***, whether you have any conscious knowledge of that pain or not.

As I described earlier, the pelvis holds tremendous stored feelings. This part of our body is often referred to in poetry, literature and drama as our *dark, murky nether regions* – mysterious, dangerous, sexual, warlike. Remember your trip to the zoo. Those powerful urges imprinted in our DNA – clearly *primitive and primal* – are terrifying to most of us. They defy logic. They fly in the face of all the efforts that went into turning us all into *civilized* creatures. They are also that which makes an *actor* electrifying! Your chest, hands, face and stomach are now ready to welcome these darker more primitive feelings.

- Once again, place one hand in the centre of your chest, making contact with your broken heart, and the other either on your upper or lower abdomen, saying hello to all your fears.
- **We will begin to wake up the pelvis by making circular movements** – these will feel slightly ridiculous, or sexy, or stiff

and hard to do. Just explore. If it begins to feel 'dirty,' you are
doing it right.

- You'll recognize that this movement is not dissimilar to the
  sexy hip gyrations when you dance at a club. Ah, I think you're
  getting the idea. Hopefully, you're smiling. All you're doing now
  is finding the coordination we want with this movement. Your
  arms and hands are protecting you as you move. It's fine to feel
  slightly foolish.

- If these movements are difficult and feel *as though you are
  moving through cement* you know that you've developed strong
  muscular control over your rage. Great discovery. Just keep
  urging your muscles to permit you to move.

- Once you've established the movements in your pelvis, **raise
  your arms to shoulder height and push them straight out
  in front of you, flexing your hands strongly at the wrists
  so your palms are facing outward**. In this position your arms
  are saying, *'You can't get any closer than this unless I give you
  permission.'* This is a powerful primal statement.

- Now you can add pelvic thrusts to the circular movements
  and see how that feels. Open your jaw wide and take a sharp
  inhalation. **There is a direct connection between the back
  of the throat and the movement of the pelvis.** You might
  feel a surge of energy – or a ripple of feeling.

- **Stamp your feet whenever you feel yourself getting tight.**
  Children love to stamp their feet. It makes a wonderful loud
  noise and feels powerful. (It is also an instinctive way to release
  any tightness in the legs that signals to the tightness in the
  pelvis.) How long has it been since *you* stamped your foot?

- Next, while you're moving your pelvis I want you to draw your
  hands back near your body, bending your elbows, so you
  can then **thrust your arms vigorously out in front of you
  and say, 'No!'** in a loud voice while your arms are making
  that *pushing away* motion. This is very nourishing and totally
  instinctive. You can repeat this several times. 'No! No! No!'

- Don't be surprised if your pelvis stops moving when you add
  the arms thrusting forwards – it's just a matter of practice and

reminding the pelvis to join the act. **We are awakening the instincts to fight back.** Sometimes the circular movements don't work and just pelvic thrusts feel more natural – explore, see where your body takes you.

Your Intellect would probably love to stop and analyze all of this. Try to ignore it! I am hoping you received little glimmers of feelings, slight trembling in your hands or face. You may also experience changes in your breathing. *Your emotions are being invited to come out of the Dungeon to play.*

Take a break, jump around. Stamp your feet. Try not to analyze anything or listen to your Intellect telling you this is all too bizarre. We will now go through each of these steps, *without explanations, adding words which I will prompt so we can avoid the Intellect's interference.* This will most closely approximate your personal *self-tuning*. You'll find that after you practise this a few times, you will have very quickly memorized it. *Your muscles are learning this process even more quickly than your mind.* But, please, do not expect big surges of emotion at first. For years your feelings have been told to hide or to 'act'. They will learn to trust they can be heard *if you don't force them*.

You can now see why I asked you to memorize, or at least look at, those short pieces. They contain a range of human emotions. If I asked you to speak a 'sad phrase', guess who would be right there giving you 'helpful suggestions'? Your Intellect, of course! That's why we're going to go directly into your deep storage memory so these words can connect directly to your Dungeon. If you're following my audio 'cues' I will be feeding those phrases directly to you and your unconscious as well.

Whether you are working in a group or alone, it will be *tempting to your Intellect* to try to decide who you are speaking to in those short emotion-laden pieces. Resist! *Those words will connect with feelings beyond logic or memory if you permit them that freedom.* Think about the crazy things that come up in dreams – a person you haven't thought of in years, odd fragments you don't recognize. That is your Dungeon while you sleep.

Are you ready to go through this now, without explanation, just experiencing the feelings as they come?

EXERCISE

Your *self-tuning* sequence

1   Stand with your best alignment, having space around
    you. Check your feet, your arms at your sides and your
    open chest.

2   One at a time, rest the palm of your hand against the
    muscles between chest and shoulder. Breathe deeply as
    you say hello to each of these Guardians of the Broken
    Heart muscles.

3   Place one hand at the centre of your chest – your broken
    heart, one on the stomach – all your terror. Breathe.

4   Reach up and touch the muscles around your mouth,
    light as a feather.

5   Touch the muscles under your eyes, your bravery
    muscles. Stroke your eyebrows and the muscles
    between them, and your forehead and cheeks and neck.

6   Tap your chin to signal opening wide. Take a sharp
    breath to feel your throat open and release a voiced sigh.
    'Ah-h-h-h.'

7   Reach your hands out in front of you, opening and
    closing your fists. Let your hands continue to move, and
    say, 'Please, I love you.' (Don't worry if your hands
    tremble or get tight – they are responding to all those
    feelings.) Follow my prompts.

8   As you feel the crack in the Dungeon door, you can
    always move your hands back to your face, your
    stomach or chest to explore how touch can
    also enhance feelings. If you begin to tense, just
    wiggle your body, walk around at bit, pause the
    audio and then continue when you're ready. Say one
    of the poems.

9 With your back strong, reach your hands out in front of saying, 'You can't get any closer than this, unless I give you permission.'

10 You are now protected and can move your pelvis, first in circular movements, then adding pelvic thrusts. Open your jaw and throat. Take a big full inhalation of breath.

11 Begin bending your elbows and pushing your arms straight out, saying, 'No!', 'No more!' Either continue with your pelvic thrusts or circular movements – whichever feels more comfortable. Let the energy of those words support the movement. Say one of the poems.

12 Say one of the poems as we explore phrases that might connect to many of the deeply illogical, primitive feelings in your Dungeon.

13 We will now begin to pull all of this together. With your hands securely placed on your chest and stomach, say, 'This is my body! You will never hurt me again. It's my turn!'

14 Then reach one hand at a time high up, reaching away from your body, and grab a big handful of air. Then take that fisted hand back and place it at the centre of your body. As you do this, say: 'I TAKE!' (Ah, the delicious greed in every child!)

15 Repeat this action at least twice with each hand. Be sure you can feel that fisted hand touch your body.

16 Next reach both arms out just below shoulder level as though you are embracing an audience of 1,000 loving spectators. With your chest wide open, say: 'I WANT!', 'I WANT IT ALL!'

17 Move your hands back to your broken heart and stomach, and with your pelvis making circular movements, say, 'THIS IS MY BODY. YOU WILL NEVER HURT ME AGAIN. I AM STRONG NOW. I CAN FIGHT BACK NOW! NOW I CAN WIN!'

18   You can turn off the audio and explore speaking the little poems from memory or just follow my prompts as I might suggest phrases like, 'I can't carry you around any more. I'm not a transportation system.' And, 'You touch and I will kill you.'

19   Finally, for the pure joy of it, say, 'No more guilt!' Or, as some actors prefer, you can say, 'Fuck guilt!'

20   Throughout this process you can pause the audio whenever you want or **follow my cues from the online audio guide from beginning to end**. You decide what is serving you and your needs. I will pause to give you a chance to repeat my words, and leave you on your own when you are doing your monologues.

21   **Your instincts will want you to be influenced by my voice and inflection – let that happen! We are trying to shut out the Intellect.** All of your training and your desire to be wonderful will be urging you to makes these phrases interesting and full of meaning. You will want to 'act' them, 'inflecting' them skilfully. By simply following the impulses in my voice we will be making it harder for your Intellect to 'direct' and 'criticize'. Trust that you don't have to look for 'meaning' or ask whether a phrase resonates with any of your experiences. The connections we are looking for are beyond your conscious knowledge.

22   With your chest open, stretch your arms wide, as though you could touch the walls on either side of the room. Let your hands speak of needs with little fist and open movements, move your pelvis with circular or pelvic thrusts and begin speaking one of your monologues. *This is not a performance!* You are exercising your instrument. Explore! Dare to just see what happens.

The first time you do your monologues or songs your Intellect will want to tell you that you aren't ready or some other nonsense. Just dive in and, **no acting**, please. Just say the words. The words will make the connections in your Dungeon *where the feelings are waiting to speak*.

If your arms get tired of reaching, **nestle them into your body**. Place one hand at your heart, the other at your solar plexus, and *continue opening and closing your hands* as they snuggle against your body. You are invigorating your 'emotions on cue' connections. Try, please try, not to judge. 'Oh, it was better in the last monologue, not so good this time.' Silly! This is just exercise.

If you are in a group, speak directly to your fellow actors. That means you might be looking right into your friend Albert's eyes, saying, 'I love you. Please don't leave me. I'll die.' Once your Intellect quiets and your unconscious connects with those feelings, it will all make sense *inside you*. Albert is receiving those words and you are speaking them.

Even with your group as your audience, this is not yet performance. Your role in this *self-tuning* is merely to experience the *natural connection between words and emotions*. Some of the words might stir delicate or big feelings in your unconscious mind. Some may not stir any. There is no right or wrong. **You have entered moment-to-moment aliveness – your territory of disobedience!**

5

THE SUBTLE CUES FOR *RE-TUNING*: THE GREAT BALANCING ACT

You've now had your first taste of how the body can connect you to feelings when you speak memorized text. I hope you're buzzing with questions. 'Does this mean I *tune* myself every day? Can I do it for auditions? How do I keep getting better at this? What's my next step?'

First of all, this is only the beginning! Just as you wouldn't assume that you could go from lifting one kilo weights to fifteen kilos after a couple of days; *over time you will build incredibly strong neuromuscular connections*. The more you do this work, the easier and more instantaneous it will become. So, when do you *tune* yourself? When you are going to act, of course!

If you want a *daily routine* I heartily recommend you do some nourishing *physical* activity: yoga, running, dance, Pilates (or a combination of them!) and *a good voice warm up*. You need your voice and body to be flexible and strong. Those muscles respond very well to daily exercise – providing you with the ability to respond to any impulses from your Dungeon.

Access to your Dungeon has already begun. You will *tune* yourself:

- As you work through the different chapters in this book.
- If you are getting together with friends to do monologues.
- To prepare for improvisations.

- If you are in rehearsal and you are working on scenes or doing run-throughs where you are 'off book'.

- If you want to work on a monologue by yourself, know it solidly, and then explore it emotionally.

- Always before a performance.

- As your 'preparation' in an acting class

- Always before each take when filming.

- Just for the fun of it.

- Always before an audition.

You have a powerful tool. **The more you use it, the more quickly and intuitively you will make those connections.** Once again, you are creating circuits in your brain and conditioning your muscles to *respond to touch and movement*. The good news is once you are accustomed to it, *being in your body* usually takes less than a minute.

Yes, you read that correctly. *Less than a minute*. Many actors find their Dungeon popping open within seconds! The brain-body connection works *lightning fast*. Many of you are used to long *preparation*, taking ten, twenty minutes or longer.

I'm afraid that the most bewildering thing about *acting with passion* is that it seems to be TOO EASY. And that will drive you crazy for a while. We are all so used to *working* at acting. The Intellect is always so anxious to tell us it's 'not good enough' if we aren't making *massive efforts*.

'If I *tune* in the morning will it last for an afternoon audition?'

Whether you have an audition late in the afternoon or a rehearsal in the evening I recommend you do your *self-tuning* in the *privacy of your home* (or your dressing room) before you set out for your day. Don't worry if this is early in the morning and you have hours ahead at your day job. Remember, this process is not about some form of 'concentration' where you have to *hold thoughts in your head* – an almost impossible task.

Once you've established those brain-body connections early in the day, you'll find that all you need to do is give yourself little 'cues' to reawaken them. I will talk you through this whole process, including these 'cues'. Because this tuning takes place *on a physical level and not a mental level*, your *muscles will hold the messages of release and connection to feelings that are waiting to be reawakened*.

At first you will be looking for 'results'. I'm afraid that's the tyranny of your Intellect. *Try to tune yourself with simple curiosity*. I would love you to think, 'I wonder what feelings want to come out to *play* once I open my Dungeon?' Having your *emotions on cue* is really just a matter of being in your body with the Dungeon open. **The words of your text will call out to the feelings inside you** and will **immediately surround those words with feelings.** Often ones that surprise you.

Yes. Your emotions have been held prisoner by the Intellect. They are eager to escape. Like children being kept still in a stuffy classroom, they are all longing to run about, to express themselves and to play! Trust that it *will always be the words you speak* that will create the connections you want. But be careful that you don't demand your emotions to 'perform'. It's tempting to want gushing tears and roaring rage. Remember, you are only wanting to crack open the Dungeon door. *Your words will take care of the size and shape of the emotions.*

The child voice

One practical way to *damp down those expectations* is *to really try to use a child-like voice* when you warm up with most of those phrases and short pieces. Obviously this *confuses your Intellect* and thus makes it easier for you to be open to whatever happens. You can't do your usual 'clever line readings' or 'emotional pushing' when your voice is in this range. I promise you, when you go to act at an audition or performance you will speak in your normal range! **We are using this as a tool to facilitate access to your *unconscious*.** Your 'child voice' holds a *great deal of emotional circuitry in the way it triggers various muscles in the throat and vocal cords*.

The child voice utilizes the upper range of your vocal cords. This is the area where the cords are thinner, closer together and vibrating at the fastest speeds. On our mind-body level the use of this voice sets off reverberations on several different sensory paths and connections to the unconscious.

- The musculature around the vocal cords holds a remembrance of those high infant cries, *alerting the unconscious*.
- Feedback from your auditory neurons signals 'child feelings'.
- The muscular controls in the throat are *deactivated* since this voice seems to pre-date the development of the throat armour.
- The sounds are actually *healthier*. When the vocal cords vibrate this quickly there is less chance for air to pass through causing calluses (nodes) and roughness for the cords. Babies can cry for over an hour and never get hoarse.
- The learned bravery, *adult child act* and other vocal repertoires are set aside allowing the feelings to flow.

You'll even find this exploration of the high notes (falsetto for men) will *increase and energize your speaking voice range*. A good voice teacher will encourage you to expand your vocal range, supporting these efforts. Finally, for the health of your voice, when you are exploring your rage and want to shout many of the phrases in those short pieces, you will not be in any danger of hurting your throat.

Not looking for a specific emotion

Let's say you're going to audition for Coriolanus: it seems natural to say to yourself, 'I must *tune* myself to connect to my rage.' That is a trap. As soon as you decide you are looking for a *specific emotion* the Intellect is on high alert, at the Dungeon door just waiting for that rage to *dare to emerge*. Out comes the whip, pushing that rage down and then *encouraging you to churn and manufacture emotions instead*.

Crazy, huh? But you already instinctively understand this. You know the bullying of your Intellect telling you, 'Now you need anger. Now you need sadness.' How *impossible* does it become when the Intellect is directing the show?

Remember *you are merely opening the Dungeon*. All of your emotions live in there together, bumping up against each other. Rage is next to joy, next to sadness, next to fear, abandonment, embarrassment, sexiness, vengeance, you name it. When you *tune* yourself you are just opening the door and *inviting your feelings to join with the text*. Quite often you will only experience *a tiny 'thrill'* in the centre of your body where you feel totally alive. That's perfect. Your Dungeon is open. The feelings are then free to connect to the words – beyond any logic or 'direction' your Intellect can offer.

It might be a pretty, sunny day and you feel great. You open your Dungeon and happiness, lightness, maybe giggles start to bubble up. That's okay. Please don't worry. If you are playing Medea, the moment you say, 'Jason' everything will shift. The words of your text and the given circumstances contact *all* your feelings. The fury and jealousy of Medea will be hard to hold back.

This is a new way of working, without figuring out in advance, 'I need to be sad here. I need to be angry on that line.' It feels at first as though you are walking a tightrope without a safety net. *In exchange for the certainty of all that pre-planning, you have the exhilarating experience of truly living moment to moment*. Generally your director will be delighted with such spontaneity.

'So what *exactly* should I do when I *tune* myself?'

For now, please reread the last chapter whenever you want to remind yourself of this process in full detail. The first few times you will probably use my audio prompts, but very quickly you will have memorized the sequence. Try not to dwell on each step, letting your Intellect question, 'Is that it? Am I feeling the Dungeon open?' Your Intellect is not really invited to this party! So don't listen to it. Your body is responding and stirring your unconscious. Ultimately you will find that *the connections happen very quickly*. I believe your feelings say, 'Whoopee! We're going to get out to play,' with the very *first cues*.

Ultimately, you will do your own version of that chapter. It will become *your personal self-tuning*. You will sense what is working best for you and your body. Just as one more reminder, you and I will go through the process right now. I will be prompting you with new and different phrases. You and I will 'play' together now. **[https://vimeo.com/102846841]**

EXERCISE

- **Alignment:** standing with your feet parallel, a little wider than hip-width, check your alignment. Chest open, shoulder blades nestled into your back. Pelvis free.
- **Guardians of the Broken Heart:** one at a time rest the palm of your hand on these delicate muscles. Breathe!
- **Broken heart and stomach/fear:** rest your hands on your broken heart and all the fears in your stomach.
- **Mouth and eyes:** lightly brush the muscles around your mouth and then around your eyes, eyebrows, face and neck.
- **Opening the throat:** tap your chin to open your mouth and jaw. Sharp inhalation as the throat opens. Release a voiced sigh.
- **Hands speaking of needs:** reach your arms out and let your hands open and close, signalling needs. Look at your hands, really see them and release a voiced sigh.
- **Child voice:** say, 'I'm frightened, I need you.' Or speak any of the phrases you've learned. Or just follow my prompts.
- **Protection against pain:** turn your palms out, arms straight – *'You can't get any closer than this unless I give you permission'* – position. Say, 'Don't touch me!'
- **Pelvis and rage:** move your pelvis, circular motion, and release your jaw. Shout, 'No!'
- **Arms push away protection:** draw your elbows back and then shoot your arms straight. Say, 'Get away! Leave me alone!' as you thrust those hands out to protect you. Or use my prompts.
- **Vocal release:** you can shout a big, 'NO more!' Let these vowels really resonate.

- **Ownership:** hands again on heart and stomach, you say, **'THIS IS MY BODY. YOU WILL NEVER HURT ME AGAIN!'**
- **I take:** grasp and return hand to your solar plexus as you say, 'I TAKE!' Repeat with other hand.
- **I want:** arms stretched out wide on either side of you as you say, **'I WANT!'** With your arms embracing a vast audience and your chest wide open, say **'It's my turn to win!'**

Leaving your arms outstretched let your hands fist and open and your pelvis move while you do a monologue or song, and enjoy how open you feel. *You can do a monologue or song, or a couple of the short pieces you've memorized – try different ones each time.* Let your body movements then **become your natural gesture** – next chapter! Then off you go – whether it's to a day job or a class, you're ready to act at a moment's notice.

Because all of this takes place on a neuromuscular level, once you have opened that Dungeon, all you need to do is *'cue' your muscles again later* in the day. **Your muscles have been 'programmed' to respond.** Magic. The Dungeon flies open. I know the first few times you won't trust this completely. It doesn't seem possible that it could be that easy. But it is.

How do I cue my muscles later in the day?

I've found that actors quickly learn *their own most effective cuing by experimenting*. For a while you will probably *want* to go through practically the entire *self-tuning* again. Don't be alarmed if you don't have time or privacy. You only need a minute or two to reawaken those connections. You can duck into the ladies or gents, close the door and see what happens when you *merely touch your face, your Guardians of the Broken Heart muscles, open your jaw and throat and ask your hands to open and close.* A couple of pelvic thrusts while pushing your hands away – and I will bet you can feel your body come alive and your emotions just itching to get out.

Try not to linger with each touch so your Intellect doesn't have a chance to tell it isn't working. Just be curious and *feel the sensations of your hands making contact with your muscles and skin.* Remember the homunculus and how dominant your hands are. When they even lightly brush your neck or cheek you will begin to feel that connection. **The delicate sensory fibres of the skin are speaking directly to your Dungeon.** Don't be surprised if it just takes seconds. The muscles, deeply layered in your body, feel those delicate connections. *We have been programming them.*

Sometimes you'll be rushing to an audition and all you have time for is an open-throated breath, a quick touch of your face and maybe a hand on your tummy for a moment to connect with the fear. You can do all these cues quite subtly if you need to – sometimes in a waiting room surrounded by other actors. Your name is called, you take that lovely open throat inhale, and as you stand up make sure your hands make quick contact with your body – stomach, broken heart. No one will know what you're doing.

As you begin to experience the feeling of the Dungeon opening almost as soon as you begin to touch your body and face, you can be confident those connections are well established. You will experiment and find which things help cue you the best. For some actors, it's merely touching the stomach and heart, for others using those protective arms out straight (looks like you are having a good stretch). You can easily move your pelvis as you extend that stretch. And resist looking around for fear someone will notice. This is your secret and no one will suspect.

Explore ways to cue your muscles that are *subtle enough* to do them on a film set as you walk over to the camera, or as you go into an audition, or before your entrance onstage.

Try these – a few more ideas for you to play with. They are all effective so you can try different combinations each time.

- *Always open your jaw* (naturally, not overly wide) and take a sharp inhalation signalling your throat to open (looks like a yawn). This will have an immediate internal response within your whole body. Remember, *the back of the throat is one of the main thresholds for release of feelings* and one you learned to tighten at a very early age.

- *Touch yourself.* Either brush your hand gently across your cheek and neck (a very natural-looking gesture) or rest your hand for a moment on your broken heart. We have sensitized all these muscles so the lightest touch will activate them. Brush a hand through your hair – mustn't forget all the nerve endings in the scalp!

- As you are walking, *let your hands fist and open* a couple of times and breathe!

- Be aware of your pelvis. If you feel tension and tightness, take a deep breath again and *gently stamp each foot.* And very *subtly do a pelvic thrust.* If you are very nervous, letting your body say 'no more guilt' or even just whispering the word 'fear' will feel great. (Can't begin to tell you *how many actors* now do this on film sets and no one seems to notice.)

- You can also *dive into the bathroom/loo/toilet*, close the door and rotate your pelvis, push your arms away, fist and open your hands, breathe and enjoy your moment of privacy! You just can't *shout* 'no more guilt' or 'I want!'

When I'm *self tuning* should I try to visualize things?

NO! It is a tempting thought that when you push away and say, 'Don't touch me', you try to decide who you might say that to. It *seems logical* that you would want to visualize the people in your life when you say many of those emotional phrases. However, I'm going to remind you that we are treading a delicate path. *We are opening access to your unconscious mind – visualizing will open access to your Intellect.*

As I said, this is delicate. By offering to 'help it along' with visualization you are inviting the participation of your *conscious* mind: *your visual cortex – and the Intellect.* You are effectively shutting out the unconscious and all the feelings in your Dungeon. You are also inviting your Intellect to tell you how to make any feelings 'bigger and better'. *Just let your eyes see whatever they see* – your unmade bed, the window, the wall, your desk piled high with work to do. Anywhere you gaze will receive the words you are saying.

If you are at home, or have complete privacy after you've opened your Dungeon, enjoy it. *Do a monologue, song, visit an old monologue and see what happens.* Then off you go – whether it's to a rehearsal or a class, you are ready to act at a moment's notice.

Always in a group make eye contact with your fellow actors. This is very important. Alone, *I want you to open your eyes to look at your hands when first you reach out to let them express 'needs'.* Then just permit your gaze to fall anywhere.

Once you touch your muscles, move and speak, that powerful visual sense will probably recede. If I asked you what you were looking at when you said, 'I love you' you probably wouldn't have any recollection. Great! When the unconscious is free to roam we can *see effortlessly* without consciously *noting* what we are looking at.

If you have a practice group, of course they can terrifically support your *self-tuning*. Really looking into their eyes and saying such emotion-laden phrases can be profound – given how much we've learned to hide. Some of you have probably been given criticism from acting teachers in the past for not looking directly into people's eyes. You now understand that it was *because you were desperately hiding in your fortress*.

There is *no real danger* in the room as you work with your friends on all of these concepts – those danger signals are coming from your 'child intellect', remember. I'll remind you that at first you will have concerns about speaking those short poems while looking at each other. *The words feel so intimate.* You aren't revealing anything about yourself other than the fact that you are a talented actor with access to a range of feelings. The odd thing is that after a moment or two the brain has no problem with you saying, 'I will hate you forever!' with vehement emotion as you look directly at a dear friend. (Not unlike what actors are asked to do all the time. The actor-friend backstage is also the character we might try to kill every night and then hug after the curtain call!)

Really 'seeing' versus ' visualizing'

How much simpler it is for the actor to rely on the extraordinary gifts the brain possesses rather than its limitations. The *acting with passion* path is *to always let yourself really see whatever is really there*. You are looking at 'dear Albert' again, as Clytemnestra screaming for his death. Of course you see him! This is called theatre, you aren't trying *to see* Agamemnon – and Clytemnestra doesn't really kill Agamemnon each night. The re-casting would cost a fortune. The glorious world of your illogical Dungeon – where our madness lives – seems to have no problem with this 'bending of reality'.

Meisner's brilliant creation, the repetition exercise, captures this concept perfectly. So, you are seeing whatever is actually there. How do you deal, then, with all the instructions you've been given about the need for 'visualization'? We've been led to believe that if I say, 'My beautiful cherry orchard!' and *I don't visualize those pink blossoms*, how can the audience possibly see that image?

Oh, you are ahead of me! You remember from the *emotions on cue* chapter all the brain mechanisms that make visualization so problematic! Think of all of the effort we have all put into trying to make it work. **Nothing trumps reality!** If you are *really seeing something* the audience sees you – **in the moment** – really using the powerful visual sense. If you are asking your brain instead to *recreate an image of trees and blossoms*, **it means you are not in the moment at all**.

If the cherry orchard has been 'placed' in the audience for example, you would be looking out at the back wall of the theatre, *treasuring the exit signs, the bricks, the doors* – all of the real things that back wall contains. And as you *say the words, 'My beautiful cherry orchard' your Dungeon will supply all the rich feelings you could ever ask for*. Might your brain flash an image? Yes, probably. And if you are in a long run, each night you might get a different image, or some nights none at all. And it won't make a difference!

If we just use the brain the way it is designed, it means *seeing whatever you are really seeing* in front of your eyes. The more you really see what is there the more you have liberated your wonderful brain to do what it does intuitively. It will flash pictures, flying past – the brain 'thinks in pictures' not in words. When you say, 'My beautiful cherry orchard', the brain may show you a palm tree while you gaze at the back wall of the theatre. And, at the same time your Dungeon will surround the words, 'cherry orchard' rich with emotion.

I want you to trust this same concept when you are on camera. Whether you are speaking directly to the lens or at a mark on a piece of paper near the lens, you will be *really seeing it, not pretending the camera is your best friend, not imagining your lover's face, not acting*. I will be discussing this in greater detail in the auditions chapter.

The delicious problem opening your Dungeon can present

When you *tune* yourself you can predict that you will be in touch with feelings, *but how much and which ones might assert themselves is often a surprise*. I believe there is nothing more pleasurable than having your emotions take you by *surprise* when you are acting! (As they do in life.)

As you explore your various monologues, scenes and performances you will experience this again and again. This means that there will be times when your Dungeon will feed you *more emotion than is actually right for the play or that moment in the play*. That isn't your signal to shut down your Dungeon! **See what happens if, instead, you let your character deal with those emotions.** Maybe the character will choose to be brave, or angry, instead of tearful. How exciting for the audience to watch the character 'handle the feelings' as we all do in life.

Your job is to tune your instrument, right? That makes all those feelings 'available'. **Then it is your character's job to *deal* with them.** We do this all the time. You give me some 'constructive criticism'. I immediately feel hurt and tears begin to gather in my throat. I deal with this by gulping down those tears, smiling, and saying, 'Thank you so much. I really appreciate your advice.' I have *chosen* in that moment to hide my hurt feelings. *This is exactly what your character can choose to do at any moment.*

In fact, seeing your character be brave is often much more moving than seeing him give in to feelings completely. The camera seems to really love bravery where we can see those glimmers of the heartbreak underneath.

'How do I keep going deeper?'

Actors often ask how they can keep opening up more and more feelings. At the beginning they are pleased to get access to any emotions, but they know there are many more still hidden deep inside. Once again, the Intellect's advice would be to push the feelings you have access to and make them bigger.

I obviously don't agree. Your feelings need to be given words to speak. You have at your fingertips a most extraordinary range of plays and screenplays. *You can explore any feeling that interests you.* I want you to be like a 'kid in a candy store', hungry to taste all the delights. Memorize as many monologues as you can. You want to explore your rage? Choose a monologue where the character can vent anger and hatred. You want delicate feelings? Choose monologues that exercise those feelings.

I always recommend that actors get acquainted with ancient Greek drama. If that sounds intimidating, you are in for a treat. If the translation is good, the language should be *very easy to understand*. The best thing about Greek drama is that **the emotions are enormous. And the rage is *guilt free*.** You can't get better than that!

Whatever play or character attracts you, *memorize the words and then let them reach into your Dungeon and inspire those feelings to come out and play*. Does it sound scary not to *know* exactly what will happen each time?

You are embarking on an adventure. That's because *acting in this way means trusting your talent*, your natural creativity and your unique brand of magic. I don't deny that the first few times it will feel like doing a high-wire act without a safety net.

The first time a film director says, 'Great. Perfect. We need another take or two, *exactly the same*, to be sure we're covered,' your heart will sink, and you will think, 'I can't repeat that exactly.' Of course not! You will open your Dungeon and let your feelings contact the words. It will certainly be slightly different, but equally alive. I believe then it is the director's and the editor's problem. I hope each take they say, 'Wow!

That's great. And that's great! And that one's super.' Then they can choose the one that best serves the film.

The more you have learned to trust your *Intellect's instructions* – especially if you have been successful using that approach in your acting career – the more this will feel dangerous. An actor I worked with left the class unconvinced that he could possibly do this before a big audition. His agent called with a casting for a West End leading role. He cursed me saying, 'That cow, Niki Flacks, tells me to risk everything and try something new for this important audition. I can't do it.' But when the day arrived he found himself *self-tuning* at home that morning and then stamping his foot just before he hit the stage. **He got the part. And so will you!**

The great balancing act

Which brings us to an intriguing issue. We know that for thousands of years people have sought to unlock the mysteries of the mind. The ancient yogis, over 5,000 years ago were experimenting with ways to 'still the chattering mind' so they could meditate. Hatha (physical yoga) as we know it today grew out of their understanding of the connection between the mind and the body. If they were focusing on holding a challenging pose, the mind could still. They called this 'moving meditation'. I believe it's one of the things we yoga aficionados treasure: the feelings of well-being and peace when we leave a good class. We have truly been 'in the moment', not dwelling on the future or past.

Today we are surrounded by all these kinds of efforts. I've become fascinated with the tight connection we actors have to the issues that face athletes. All major competitors have sports psychologists who work with them to keep their Intellects at bay. You can see a tennis player miss a shot and observe the tension that ripples through the body. As they examine their racquet they are probably working on some mantra to steady themselves, and shut out the messages of gloom and doom coming from the Intellect.

I watched an interview with a prominent golfer who put it beautifully. The golf pro explained, 'I must make the conscious decisions about what club to use, gauging the distance I need to cover and studying the course hazards.' (All of that brilliant prefrontal cortex at work!) He continued, 'At the same time I need to shut out the messages of fear that cause tension. The trick is, that once I've assessed the technical issues, I stand with the club in my hand, remember to breathe and *then give everything over to my body to just execute all of the hours and hours of practice.*' You can actually see his body shift into this other mode: not relaxed so much as fully alive. His breathing is steady. You can also see how deeply emotional he becomes. After a very important win, he was sobbing as he embraced his caddy and family. He knows how to open his Dungeon.

One cannot deny that we need the conscious mind a great deal! What we don't want is the Intellect. (And remember, the Intellect is only a small part of our wonderful conscious mind.) Of course this is exactly the same for an opera singer whose conscious mind is reminding her that the 'high C' will need a big breath beforehand, then a decrescendo into a pianissimo and must be held for six beats. And, while holding and supporting that gorgeous musical line, the body must permit the emotions of heartbreak to surround that note.

Later on I will be discussing the challenges of doing style, comedy and character. You will be reminded of the same conscious mind/Intellect/Dungeon balancing act. Many of my ideas will sound very 'technical' to you. But just like that golf pro, or the opera singer, **your brilliant mind can do all of it**. It's mainly keeping out the treacherous Intellect. *That's why I urge you to trust your body connections* as they will not let you down.

Not only are we constantly having to balance the contributions of the conscious mind while trying to quiet the Intellect; within our unconscious/Dungeon there are other partnerships at work. Think about this. You study for a history exam – prefrontal cortex, conscious mind learning. That night, your dreams are filled with those dates and battlefields and kings and queens. We have only scratched the surface in our understanding of the richness we possess in the remarkable interplay between conscious and unconscious mind!

Which brings us to another 'heady issue': text analysis. You've all been well trained to comb through scripts for meanings. Some directors like to spend weeks on 'table work', plumbing the psychology and backstories of your character. They generally say, 'Now when you go to act, forget all this and it will just be there.' Good advice, *if only the Intellect hadn't been so alerted during the process*. I feel that text analysis is *Intellect candy*: 'Look at my chance to show how clever and insightful I can be!'

It's very hard then for the Intellect to let go of that power. Hard to 'forget what has been discussed'. Instead your head is filled with instructions. 'Remember that story Brenda told that really resonated with the character?' 'You aren't showing the trauma enough.' And on and on *with direction and criticism*. Oh, and that old effort coming back!

You might enjoy looking at this very short clip of Mark Rylance discussing just this issue, the popular notion of table work for rehearsal. You can access it here: http://vimeo.com/timebombpictures/review/84340431/bc2aab771b.

What if the balancing act is really easier than we think? There is a wonderful story about one of the most remarkable twentieth-century actors, Laurette Taylor. Like so many actors of the early twentieth century, she learned her craft by being part of her parents' acting company. *She received no training at all*. She learned by watching and then experimenting on her own. Every reviewer spoke of her almost magical ability to seem totally real – moment to moment filled with feeling. Late in her life she was cast as Amanda in the premiere of Tennessee Williams' *The Glass Menagerie*. Critics were ecstatic, calling it the greatest acting ever seen. At the time the Actors Studio and the Method were believed to be the only way to achieve emotional truth. In an interview, however, when she was asked what 'techniques' she used, she look bewildered for a moment. Then she replied, 'I just say the words.'

I believe that is the core of *acting with passion*. Laurette Taylor intuited it, as I think all great actors have for centuries. For me, it was a journey of study and trial and error. It has led me to believe, however, that in the end, *all you have to do is 'say the words'*. Then the intelligence of your prefrontal cortex can easily remind you that you must cross to the window on that line, be sure you are well lit by your key light, etc. *It all happens in exquisite coordination as long as you stay connected physically.*

That's why I call it the **great balancing act**. We need all the prefrontal cortex knowledge. Without it we would be bumping into walls. There's a really wonderful Ted Talk by Dr Jill Bolte Taylor, a neuroanatomist, who suffered a massive stroke at the age of twenty-eight. Her description, as she observed her stroke – with her level of knowledge, of course –

takes us through what happened when her left brain was shut down: her language centre, her ability to reason clearly. And she describes the wonders of being in her right brain where she felt a connection to everything, everyone, every feeling. However, without the left brain she couldn't even talk on the phone to ask for help. Check it out: details are in the 'Resources' section at the end of the book.

We are all constantly learning and experimenting. Frustration or even a 'failure' may send your Intellect into overdrive. Trust your body. Say, 'No more guilt' and 'It's my turn to WIN!', and realize you just have more to explore and more to dare to attempt.

We're moving on now to **utilizing all your physical connections** so you can move onstage, in front of a camera, anywhere, engaging your body in different ways depending upon the character. All of the movements we've been practising morph into gesture. Ouch! That's another area you might have strange pre-conceived ideas about. **Hope you'll be pleasantly surprised.**

6

GESTURING: WHY SHOULD IT BE SO DIFFICULT?

'I didn't know what to do with my hands!' cries Nina in the final act of *The Seagull*. Every actor hearing this groans inwardly in recognition. We've all been there. Why is it so difficult? **We gesture constantly in life.** What happens when we get onstage?

Let's take a look at that first proposition. When you think about it you realize, of course, that *you use your hands all the time when you speak in relaxed conversation*. How often have you knocked over a water glass at dinner because you were so enthusiastically explaining something? Have you ever noticed when you are giving directions on the telephone your free hand is drawing a clear and specific map in the air even though no one can see it?

Your neuroscience insight

Neuroscience tells us our hands are connected to the language centre in the brain. Earlier I talked about how you used your hands to speak before you had any words. For years psychologists have been studying how hand movements link to the spoken word. As I mentioned in the memorization chapter when looking for a word everyone moves their fingers in small waving motions. It almost looks as though we are leafing through a dictionary unconsciously.

In a psychology study, designed to prove this phenomenon, half the 'subjects' (university psych students) were put in chairs with their hands and fingers completely unable to move. The other group were seated with their hands free to move. They were asked to respond orally to a list of definitions of various words. The subjects permitted to move their hands freely had a *significantly* higher response rate of correct answers. The unfortunate students who couldn't move their hands would find the word 'on the tip of their tongue' but then couldn't retrieve it.

Not only is the brain wiring connecting words and hand movements important for memorizing and retrieving memorized text, it is the key to why and how we naturally gesture when we communicate.

The myth about 'neutral hands'

Once again, I ask the question: if gesturing is natural in real life conversation, why do we see so many actors on stage keeping their hands pasted at their sides? To answer my question let's take a look at actor training over the past fifty to seventy-five years and how our hands have been treated.

Deeply influenced by Stanislavski as we all know, acting teachers pretty generally accepted the concept that standing with relaxed hands hanging at the sides of the body was the gold standard. (Except for the wonderful Michael Chekhov!) Stanislavski and others were reacting against the overblown melodramatic gesturing that pervaded late nineteenth and early twentieth-century acting. In trying to find more 'natural' behaviours, Stanislavski explains his work with a great opera singer given to histrionic gestures. He bound the singer's arms tightly to his sides and asked him to perform an aria. After much straining the singer broke the cords and released one powerful gesture. Stanislavski exclaimed ' Ah, that is your *one true* gesture.'

Thus drama schools began to stress the concept that standing still and finding one or two meaningful gestures would give an actor 'simplicity, strength and naturalism'. Sadly, this is has not proved to be true. Instead it has led to whole companies of armless actors, bored audiences and frustrated acting students.

The push-back I often get in talking about this comes from highly experienced, well-trained actors and directors. Their concern is that actors will instead be flinging and flailing their arms in a way that would be distracting – taking attention away from the text, especially the classics. The route I am suggesting is actually to use your hands as you do in life, as a means of *clarifying your thoughts and words*. I believe this ultimately helps illuminate text. Your character and costume will determine how expressive, extravagant or withheld the gesturing is.

Try this experiment. Stand up in front of some of your friends and describe an action film you saw recently. Keep your hands at your sides in that 'neutral' way you were taught at drama school. Be really disciplined about this, not permitting your hands or arms to leave your side – just as you were instructed – even as you feel the urge to let your hands move. First you will feel incredibly unnatural, but after a few minutes, *if you haven't warned your friends about the experiment*, they will tell you how odd and stiff you look.

In fact, if you were to meet a person who stood in the way so many of us were trained to stand onstage, you would think them horribly strange and uptight. When I demonstrate this in front of a class, within thirty seconds the actors are weeping with laughter as they see how incredibly strange and uptight this behaviour looks in normal conversation.

Next, spend some time observing people in day-to-day situations: walking down the street wildly gesturing on their mobile phones, in cafés and pubs, queuing for a film. You'll be amazed at all the gesturing you will see, such as expressive, big gestures when people are describing all kinds of experiences they've had. You'll start to become aware of the fact that you, too, use your hands when you aren't *thinking* about it.

You are realizing that the 'armless' acting you see in so many plays and sometimes experience in yourself *has no relationship to real life*. Once again, we'll listen to Hamlet's advice that we 'hold as t'were the mirror up to Nature'. But even untrained actors can find it difficult to gesture naturally onstage. *Why is that when in life we obviously move with ease?* If it isn't totally our teachers' fault, is something else going on?

The body-brain dynamic

It's time for us to talk about the body-brain dynamic that is taking place. I will remind you of our instinctive 'fight or flight' reaction. The moment the brain gets any kind of danger message, the limbic system goes into high alert. All systems are mobilized to either fight or run away. You walk out onstage to face your audience for the first time. Fear of failure! Danger! Your heart is pounding, adrenaline is pumping through your body causing heat to rise, your throat tightens and your body is primed to run away as fast as you can. *But, of course, you can't run away*. You have to go out there and act. So your body is full of the need to fight and protect yourself from attack.

Psychologists seldom talk about that *next* instinctive response, if one cannot run away or truly fight back. The next stage is *defence and protection*. **We unconsciously protect our vital organs from attack.** It's a powerful instinct. There is danger at hand and you must shield yourself from it. Every muscle in your body begins to *contract* to prepare for violence. This signals your arms and hands to close in tightly so you are ready to survive the attack. You can often feel this contraction when you get scared. For some reason, your body doesn't feel natural, alive, easy. Instead, it is tight and everything is drawn towards your centre: hands, arms, knees often knocking together.

In that moment you have experienced the feedback loop that goes from brain to body and back again. Brain signals, 'Danger!' Body kicks in with protection, tightening the muscles for self-defence. The brain senses this tension in the body and responds with, 'Wow! We must *really* be under attack, the body is getting so closed in. Protect more!' This causes us to tighten *even more*. A vicious cycle.

Sadly, this feedback loop doesn't require *real* danger. If the brain merely *perceives* danger – critics in the audience, a teacher you want to impress, the same instinctive response occurs. When we feel 'self-conscious' we are experiencing the fear that others are looking at us and we will be judged. 'I might fail and they will hate me. Danger!' It's totally primitive and in no way logical.

Let's leave acting for a moment and go to real life. Think about behaviours at large social gatherings early in the evening where people are mostly strangers. You see men with hands in pockets, arms folded across chests, women with hands tightly clenched at their waists or clinging to thighs or purses. Handshakes are awkward and tight. A giggle, 'Where's the bar?' someone asks, desperate to have something to hold in those hands. Several hours later, after a few drinks and when people have gotten to know one another, the body language changes dramatically. You see people telling jokes, sharing funny stories, acting things out with large, open gestures. *The feedback loop is finally reversed and the limbic system knows we are safe*. How can we make that happen on cue?

Reversing the cycle

Fortunately, the feedback loop goes in *both directions* as you learned from the chapter on memorization. Once again you are going to *signal your brain that you are safe*, quieting the limbic system alarms and permitting your body to feel relaxed and free. In your *self-tuning* you have, in fact, been creating a whole vocabulary of gesture. This vocabulary quite naturally reverses the feedback loop and permits you to move freely.

We talked about how important it is to open your chest and stretch your arms into a large embrace, exposing your broken heart, as when you say, 'I want!' You've also practised placing your arms straight out in front of you with the palms facing out. (Your body position is saying, 'You can't get any closer than this unless I give you permission.') You've sensed how strong you feel in both of these postures. We were not only contacting your emotions but **we were also laying the groundwork for an endless variety of gestures you want when you are acting**.

Think of your Dungeon as body centre. The closer in and more tightly held your arms and hands are to body centre the more danger your brain will sense. The further away those hands go from body centre the stronger the safety messages to the brain. It's really pretty amazing that within a second or two of having your hands move out in space you will feel a sense of physical ease. The brain seems to say, 'Wow! We must not be under attack because look how open we are. Cool.' Actors constantly tell me that when they make this adjustment they feel a remarkable shift almost instantly – a terrific sense of freedom.

At first it will take your *conscious demand*. 'I must get my arms unglued from my sides and move them out into space.' Once they are released, you'll be surprised at how quickly they want to move and help clarify what you are saying.

Some of the best advice I ever got in my acting career came when I was being fitted for a period gown by a world-famous costume designer who said, 'When you wear this bodice you must always let your armpits breathe.' One could hardly have better acting advice for *almost every* costume!

A very easy cue to regulate the feedback loop: if you feel your upper arms glued to your torso, you need to let your armpits breathe!

On a brain level, the message from the body is, 'We're not under attack. We're safe and therefore can move freely.' The limbic system registers this shift and eases off with the danger message. The more you move around, the more open your gestures become, the more you will feel the tension soften and the terror retreat.

You can experiment with this. Go back to tight muscles, pulling your arms close into your body, as though you need to protect yourself. You'll begin to feel that immediate push from your unconscious to tighten even more. Your heart rate will accelerate. You'll feel your diaphragm become rigid and your breathing shallow. By *purely physical cues* you can really work yourself into full-blown terror!

Time to explore

With this in mind, let's play for a moment or two. Ask a friend or fellow actor to stand three or four feet from you, facing you. *Take turns describing your kitchens*. Realize that you usually (in life) describe things while still looking back and forth at the other person's face rather than dramatically trying to do a pantomime of your detailed visualization. In life, *eye contact is our way to check if the other person is understanding – seeing* what we are describing. That also means being willing to gesture in front of you as you would if you were in a real conversation. You describe things all the time. **Don't try to visualize anything.** Just describe your kitchen and see what happens. (Your visual cortex will be sending you images that last less than a seventeenth of a second. This is so effortless you might not even be conscious of these images.) Don't let your Intellect tell you this is hard.

What did you *observe* watching your partner? After you both got over the initial self-consciousness did you find that it looked like normal conversation? If you wanted to explain that you have a window above your kitchen sink, you would not be very likely to stand stock still with your hands at your sides. **Did you notice that you found your**

hands actually moving and 'showing' your friend without your having to visualize every step of the way? That is because *your brain visualizes constantly at lightning speed*. Your demanding that it visualize something specific – show me my sink – just slows it down and forces you into effort! Your hands, when working freely with your brain, can respond instinctively to those images as they flash across your brain.

In fact our hands react to the visual images in our brain *before* we speak the words. You see a taxi with its light on. Do you shout 'Taxi!' and *then* raise your arm? Of course not. Your hand goes up the instant you see the light and your voice follows as you call out.

In light of what you've just observed I think it's time to put away a concept that became embedded at so many drama schools. One of the quickest ways to stifle any impulse to move and gesture freely was for a teacher to say, you are 'indicating' or 'demonstrating', meaning you were using gestures to show something. This was about the worst indictment possible. It accused you of using *artificial* gestures like old-fashioned *externalized* acting. You have now seen for yourself that we human beings draw very specific pictures in space constantly – showing your partner in vivid detail how the cabinets opened above the sink in your kitchen. **In life we 'indicate' like mad!** I watched a small child showing her father a newly-emerged tulip – with wonder she shaped her hands as though holding a precious tulip-shaped bowl and said, 'Flower!'

One step closer to performance

The next step, of course, is to integrate this *natural gesturing* into your acting. Either by yourself, or better still, with a few actor friends, I'd like you to take turns describing the list below to each other. These are not necessarily things you have experienced first hand. That is never a problem. Your extraordinary brain is filled with images of *all* of these things. *The remarkable truth is that once there is an image in your brain of something, your hands can describe it.* The image might come from a fifteen-second television advertisement you've seen once. Irrelevant. The hands will instinctively paint a picture in space to help you describe the image.

As a child you did all this without thinking about it. Even if you'd never picked up a heavy box in your five years of life, if an adult mimed handing you an imaginary heavy box, your arm muscles would have strained automatically in response to the image offered by the adult's body.

Trust your brain. Up on your feet. Don't listen to your Intellect when it claims you know nothing about this or that; saying, 'but you've never played tennis'. If you've seen tennis played for two minutes, you can describe it. If you're in a group, let the audience ask questions – questions that relate to the image. This will give each actor a chance to describe in even more detail. 'How tall is the net?', 'Might you aim at a target?', 'What does that target look like?'– it's not a guessing game, but an exploration of how the hands and the brain work together to explain things.

Don't be surprised if this feels unnatural at first and that 'protection of vital organs' is still going on. Just insist your hands begin to roam in space and soon they will catch up to your brain's messages of 'all clear'. Remember to let your armpits breathe!

EXERCISES

Images for you to try out describing with words and gestures

- What is a waterfall?
- What is archery?
- What is tennis?
- What is a helicopter?
- What is snow skiing?
- What is pole-vaulting?
- What is a bull fight?
- What is a parachute jump?
- What is the flying trapeze act in the circus?

What did you and your friends observe? Once you got past the initial awkwardness, I bet you all looked quite natural. Like normal, friendly, enthusiastic conversation? Was it relatively *easy* once you got over the initial *Intellect message urging caution or perfection*? Did you notice that you did not have to work at visualizing anything? The brain instantly gave you a picture or several pictures. And the more you moved your hands in space, armpits breathing, the more easily those images flew across your mind with you hardly even being aware of them.

You can add to this list any time you want to practise this crucial aspect of your acting. Take any sport you can think of and describe it in detail to a friend as though they have never seen it. I can already hear your Intellect saying to me, 'All this is fine for a modern, naturalistic play, but how would this look doing Shakespeare?' Let's take Hamlet's advice, 'Suit the action to the word.'

The last thing we want is *generalized gesturing* – usually repetitive waving arms without meaning. All of the things I've asked you to do in this chapter actually prevent that because all of these gestures are **feeding on how your hands respond *instinctively* to images in the brain**. You have just *experienced* the way your hands assist in verbalizing a concept. You are asked, 'What is football?' Your brain instantly fills with images. Your hands reach out demonstrating a large expansive field a nanosecond *before* you say, 'It's a game played on a huge field.'

When actors wave their hands around without any specific meaning they are in the grips of nervous energy, shutting out the pictures in their brain. The remedy is not to put on a straitjacket, but instead to permit the hands to *link with the words and the images in the brain*.

This intuitive link between words and hand movements is another reason why you want your text thoroughly memorized. I want you to connect with the text as easily as you did when describing your kitchen to your friend.

Our instinctive vocabulary of gesture

It's time to put this into practice with memorized text. Obviously some characters do not necessarily describe one specific image after another, while others might do just that. It depends upon the character and the script. I guess a character would describe a kitchen in detail in a scene about a new flat. As soon as I begin to talk about gesture in relating to text, everyone goes into panic mode. Actors think about line after line that seem devoid of imagery. So naturally you are thinking of pages of text without anything to describe and wondering how to apply these concepts.

First of all, you have been activating a whole range of natural gestures with your *self-tuning*. How often do you find yourself pushing your hands out in front of you, palms forward, as you say things like, 'just a minute' or 'listen to me'? It's our instinctive 'push back' gesture. Do your hands not make gentle fists, opening and closing as you reach out to someone? Just try beckoning to a child *without* using your hands in that way. And how could you possibly do the epilogue from *As You Like It* and *not* let your arms embrace the entire audience when you say, 'I would kiss as many of you . . .'?

We need to go back to looking at how the brain 'thinks'. **The brain thinks in pictures not in printed words, even when dealing with abstract information.** When I say the word *chemistry*, you do not see the word *spelled* streaking across your mind. You see pictures – not necessarily logical ones. (You might flash a picture of a dreaded high-school teacher, or a test tube. But it will be a visual image.) Because the brain also 'thinks' in terms of *time and space* you can ask anyone, 'Where do you live?' and almost everyone will respond (without even realizing they are doing it) by gesturing away from their body. No matter whether they say north, south, east or west, they will create a location in space away from their body. The brain isn't literally seeing a map of the city. Instead, an image of the flat or street is probably flashing across the mind with the spatial awareness that it is some distance away. And the hands will create the sense of that distance.

Try this experiment. *Ask for directions next time you are walking somewhere, and observe.* You can stop several people and note the different styles with which people gesture. You will certainly see that their hands immediately get involved as the need to clarify occurs – especially if you pretend to be confused: 'Is that on the right or left?' You'll see how their hands will point out things in space. This is not *pantomime*. **This is the real-life example of how hands connect to words reflecting images passing through the brain at astounding speed and placing them into spatial relationships.**

Welcome to the rich vocabulary of your gestures. So, back to the dilemma of a text seeming to be devoid of visual imagery. But wait. As soon as you reference another place – let's say the back garden – your hand will move to that location just as it did with the question 'Where do you live?' If we know from the set design that the library is 'down the hall' (stage left) and the entrance to the dining room is upstage centre, any time your character talks about an action that took place offstage in these locations *your hands will instinctively want to make some kind of reference to it*. It might only be a tiny flick of the fingers or your entire arm reaching in that direction. If you simply permit the body to react, some kind of gesture will emerge.

Doing this while you act!

Knowing now that the brain visualizes constantly I want you to take one of your monologues and decide where you might place everything you talk about. What do I mean by that? Obviously, if you are speaking *to* someone, the 'you' needs to be out front for an audition. If you are talking *about* someone, simply decide *where* that person is or was. Are they stage right? Your character remembers a trip to the seaside. Where do you want to place that fleeting image?

For a moment, let's think together about the famous speech from *Julius Caesar* that begins, 'Friends, Romans, countrymen, lend me your ears.' Playing Antony, you have many different places to reference, all of them vital: where are Brutus and the rest? Where is Caesar's corpse lying and where are the Senate House and Lupercal? Where will you place the citizens of Rome? It is through your gestures that we, the audience, *see* all these things and, quite amazingly, you will feel more connected to them as your hands reach out into space towards each of them.

A big bold movement pointing to stage left as you say, 'Thrice on the Lupercal' can express so many feelings and provides imagery for the audience who can visualize that scene as you describe it.

Once you decide where things are located, the next step is to *permit your hands to move in those various directions in response to your spoken words*. Please, hold onto the freedom you felt when your armpits were breathing and you were describing large images like waterfalls or a tennis serve. Give yourself the same generosity in your movements. Instead of placing your lover close to you, place him at the back of the theatre so you need to really *reach* out to him.

Now, am I suggesting you plan every gesture? NO! I'm suggesting, instead that you *trust your brain*. Once your brain registers locations on your *internal mapping* device your hands will instinctively move in relationship to those areas. You now understand the lightning-quick processing of your mind. You can see that if you try to 'think' your way into gesturing, instructing your hands to do this and that, *you are only slowing things down and getting in the way*. And it will be the worst kind of gesturing: artificial.

Your hands also have to rest at times

As you observe non-actors in relaxed conversation, you will notice, of course, how infrequently they have their hands at their sides. Did you notice where their hands were when they weren't actively gesturing? We don't gesture and move our hands *constantly*. Our hands respond instinctively to a need to clarify something. In between they are in a 'pause position'. Contrary to what your drama school told you, *that is not necessarily hanging at your sides*. Instead, we often seem to suspend our hands in front of us, elbows bent (but armpits not suffocated). Or they rest on our hips, arms crossed at the chest. It all depends upon your character, costume and intuitive responses. The hands may be quiet for a while – they are waiting to be called upon. They aren't limp, you will notice, but alert, 'at the ready'. Try to catch yourself in normal conversation so you can begin to *see where your hands most comfortably rest when you aren't thinking about it*.

Oddly, when you watch children before the pivotal age of seven or eight when self-consciousness first appears, you can see that they are often quite comfortable with hands at their sides. However, unlike a trained actor, their hands are quite lively. And they move away from the body instantaneously in response to what is happening. Observe small children at a playground as they group around to watch something – the construction of a sand castle, the pouring of water into a hole. You can see that their hands almost twitch in unconscious interest in what they are watching. Ah, if only we could be that completely alive and in the moment!

As adults, we need to accept our conditioning and permit our hands the freedom to behave as they do when we are *least self-conscious*. Our hands should be alert and ready to speak, even when at rest.

Time to dive in

Because you might be fighting those instinctive urges to protect yourself and free up your body, especially when you begin to perform, you need to **demand that your hands venture into space with the *first line* of your monologue**. You want that feedback loop to kick in *immediately*. Once your brain registers safety, instinct will take over. Your hands will begin to do what they normally do when you aren't on stage. Do not underestimate the power of that brain-body feedback loop! It is very sensitive to the slightest nuance of change in body tension level. One more thing to keep in mind: you won't erase years of your hands being trained to fall limply at your sides. At first you must *consciously* remind them to 'hang out' in the way you naturally do when you aren't conscious of it. Soon your hands will simply respond to your character's needs, the words spoken and your interactions with other actors.

Of course, character and costuming will ultimately drive your style of gesturing and will determine the pause position of your hands when 'at rest'. Right now we are just focusing on your ability to tap into *your core, authentic style* of movement. In the next chapter I will be discussing how much costuming affects movement and helps us to create living, breathing characters who inhabit their bodies. One of the main differentiators of a character's personality will be the style of gesture. And each period and culture, as well, offers rich constraints for actors to deal with in their movements.

For now, I'd like you to become an avid observer of how our present-day clothing influences our movements. When you are at home with your closest friends, wearing jeans and a sweatshirt, you will move and gesture differently than when you are wearing formal clothing. Become aware as you engage in different activities and watch others as they adapt their body language from situation to situation.

In a moment you need to put down the book and try all this, speaking one of your well-memorized monologues aloud. *To get your armpits breathing immediately, it is helpful to decide the direction your hands will move as you say your first words*. To whom are you speaking and where are they? **Really reach out in that direction.** Don't be surprised if you feel resistance to this. That's just *habit*. If you are speaking to the audience, it is natural to reach out in front of you. Your hands can say, 'Wait a minute, it's my turn to speak', as in Antony's oration. In which case you might find yourself using gestures similar to your *self-tuning*.

Then just wander around letting your arms and hands move freely as you speak your memorized text. Usually, once you've asked them to move in a bold way with the first few lines, the rest just falls into place naturally. But first *you need to decide on the location of the various things you will be speaking about*. Then let your instincts do the rest. Other than that, just see what your hands do when you *permit them to talk*.

If you are in a group the first time you are going to experiment with your monologues, *rehearse them all at the same time*. Walk around the room randomly, *ignoring each other*. **With all of you speaking *at the same time* no one feels as though they are being watched.** As you now know, as soon as you realize you are being observed that self-consciousness will kick in and begin to give you danger messages. After you've practised a few times with the comfort that no on is watching you (or judging you), try it out in front of someone. You will *tune* yourself to make sure your Dungeon is open – although all this physical preparation will actually invite your dungeon to open as well.

If you are working in a group of actors, great. Watch and encourage each other. When you are doing Shakespeare you will see how big bold movements suit the text. Try not to get caught in describing or acting out *every* image, like a kindergarten teacher – that's just your Intellect trying to make it 'perfect'. Trust that your hands may simply reach out as you say, 'this wooden O' rather than making the shape of an 'O'. If you are practising on your own, once you are feeling comfortable with the gestures, take a peek in the mirror or put on a video camera so you can see how you look.

Try it with a song

My final challenge for you in this arena is really going to send your Intellect into orbit. *If you think gesturing naturally with a monologue is hard, talk to singers*. The trap for anyone singing a song is that damned feedback loop combined with a lot of clichéd ideas. Actors who normally move with ease can find themselves at a singing audition standing rigidly, arms dangling with the occasional outward movement as the song climaxes.

First you must realize that *every song is really telling a story*, hopefully a personal story. And secondly, the singer must integrate movement that is visually compelling at the same time as it enhances the story-telling. It is just like a monologue, only with music. If you are finding this daunting, I'm going to suggest an exercise that will challenge you even further and **begin to shake loose all resistance to the instinctive urge to gesture**. Here's my invitation to *play*.

- I'm going to ask you to create a pantomime of something quite physical. Where you can reach up and out, away from your body. And don't freak out at the word 'pantomime' – you did this quite naturally throughout your childhood.

- Do not try to find an activity that relates to the story your song is telling.

- Once you've established the pantomime, start to *speak* the lyrics at the same time as though you are telling this story to someone in the room.

- Repeat the pantomime but the second time *sing* your lyrics.

- You might be singing a song of a lost love and pantomiming the grooming of a horse – doesn't relate at all. Just be curious and see what happens. Maybe you're doing that activity and thinking about that lost love at the same time?

- And don't forget to continue communicating the lyrics to the audience by looking at them as well as looking at your activity – splitting your focus.

Yes, it's like patting your head and rubbing your stomach. *And it's brilliant exercise for your brain*. Electrical engineers would call this 'multiplexing'.

I recommend this exercise for any of you actors who are afraid you can't sing. When I teach musical theatre classes I find the non-singers discover amazing hidden talent. By confusing the Intellect and keeping the body completely engaged you have freedom to sing and not judge every note. This crazy exercise is most fun to do in a group, where you learn so much from each other. However, it's also worth practising alone. Decide on a couple of points on a wall or pieces of furniture you are facing so you know where you will be looking when you 'talk' to your audience or the person you are singing to.

The final step is to permit the pantomime to morph into beautiful, interesting movements and gestures for your song. That's why you are looking for a pantomime that will permit you to stretch and move your hands into space. The pantomime was just to set the feedback loop and permit you to then respond more intuitively to your lyrics. Many singers find they've incorporated some of the movements from their pantomime and they work beautifully. I've found that if you choose a pantomime that is fussy and busy with too many little 'props' you might get less from it. Your Intellect may want to remind you of each little thing. That means, if you want to pantomime cooking, spend plenty of time getting ingredients out of cupboards (which you will place over your head, please). Put your work surface right in front of you, facing the audience. You want to be looking at your audience, they are the ones to whom you are telling your story. And you *happen to be cooking* (chopping, stirring, kneading) at the same time. We do this in life all the time, don't we? We have very lively conversations while we create entire meals.

I'll suggest some activities for you to try pantomiming with songs. My experience with teaching this is that the minute I describe the exercise everyone goes into brain freeze and can't think of a single physical activity.

You want to choose something that gets your hands away from your body, or permits you to touch your body in a sensual way. Once again, we are wanting to engage the *entire* body, alive, energized. You know how easy it is for the head to take over and suddenly your body feels like you are moving through cement. Fortunately, with this exercise we can keep your Intellect busy helping you to do your pantomime so it doesn't have as much chance to criticize your singing. Here are a few examples of activities that work well with song lyrics:

- Getting undressed and taking a shower – include shampooing and drying off with a big towel (this is terrific for sexy love songs).

- Packing a bag, getting clothing from wardrobe to suitcase.
- Grooming a horse, stroking its face, etc.
- Sculpting an enormous statue out of clay (taller than you are).
- Tennis (as long as you can pause every now and then, check your racquet) – the tennis serve is a wonderful movement.
- Putting up wallpaper.

Pardon me while I have a momentary rant about how many acting teachers have ruined any concept of pantomime. Too many actors have shared their frustrations as they spent hours in acting classes trying to mime holding *imaginary teacups* only to be told, 'I don't believe you. I don't believe you are really holding a cup.' What nonsense! The poor actor is trying to manipulate his brain to *see* and *feel* the cup, when of course it *isn't real*. It's a lesson in *effort* with the Intellect going wild. Bottom line, you already know how to mime anything you have seen. You have been doing this since early childhood. Invite any four-year-old to take a bite of an imaginary piece of cake and just watch them. All of you pantomimed with ease and joy before anyone told you it was a special skill. So when your Intellect tries to tell you that you *can't do this exercise*, you know that's not true.

When you're ready to adapt this pantomime into gestures to energize your song, don't choose complicated movements. Try everyday things – simple things. Let's say you mimed getting undressed to take a shower, you might begin your song with that same impulse to pull your shirt over your head. But instead of seeing you mime *accurately* we just see your arms coming up over your head expressing the thought you are singing. Your hands might even fall onto the top of your head in a feeling of wonderment or confusion – if it suits the lyric.

Don't forget that *a new thought will usually arrest a movement altogether* so your hands (as in life) become suspended in mid-action as you complete this phrase or idea. It is ultimately the *lyrics* that you must serve, just as in a monologue – the words give you the feelings. All this natural movement keeps you rooted in your body and permits you to connect to the story you are telling without your Intellect criticizing. By the way, you are welcome to try out those pantomimes with monologues as well!

Don't fight your instincts

You are wired beautifully for the task of acting. You're lucky your hands are connected to the verbal centre of the brain, that they instinctively gesture to clarify your thoughts. How amazing that our hands *want* to paint pictures in space. We are fortunate to be able to reverse the feedback loop of danger and tension and permit our bodies to behave onstage with the same freedom and ease we have in easy conversation with our best friends. **You will find there's very little more exhilarating than doing a passionate speech with your entire instrument fully engaged: voice, emotions, and body!**

7

CONSUMMATE ARTISTRY: STYLE, CHARACTER AND COMEDY

Oh, the myths that abound in areas of style, character creation and playing comedy. Like so many aspects of actor training, actors have been led to believe that these things require a *unique re-tooling* in some way. You enter a class teaching 'style' – generally associated with Restoration comedy, or Molière or some other classical playwright, and feel as though you've entered an alternative universe.

Throw out real feelings. We're in the realm of funny voices, funny faces and funny walks. What is worrying is the idea that comedy or style requires a whole different form of acting. **There are only two kinds of acting: *good and bad.*** You are either fully present, alive and in the moment, or you are not, no matter what kind of play you are performing.

Just a note: some of you reading this book will have been fortunate enough to have had superb training and/or superb experiences with all three of these challenges. Many of the top tier drama schools cover these brilliantly. You can read through this chapter enjoying the pieces that offer you additional food for thought. If any of these concepts are new to you, then I urge you to explore them with pleasure.

What essentially is style?

In general terms style means demonstrating something other than naturalistic, present-day behaviours. Did Marie Antoinette behave (walk, gesture, sit, stand) differently than we do today? Absolutely! She had to carry around a three-foot tall wig on her head to begin with. She wore a tight corset and a pannier that meant she bumped into things closer than at least four feet on either side. But did she experience emotions differently than we do? I don't believe she did. She was a spoiled, frivolous woman but she *felt* sadness, fear, anger, disappointment, just as all of us do today. (I hope you are thinking: her brain connections would have been the same as ours, her limbic system and prefrontal cortex operating exactly as yours and mine.)

When you break down the elements that comprise an actor's *embodiment* of another period you realize that it mostly comes down to clothing. What we wear dictates a great deal about how we move and interact physically with the world around us. I look back at my own training and some of the actor training currently offered and am amazed at how much more complicated everyone wants to make it.

In fact, classes in style are often intimidating and confusing. Actors in trainers (sneakers) and blue jeans prancing around with handkerchiefs trying to whirl and twirl to 'say' something – one teacher claims there's a whole vocabulary behind the twirls of the handkerchief. No one seems to mention *why* everyone carried this ornament in the seventeenth and eighteenth centuries. People carried a handkerchief, heavily doused with perfume, so they could wave it in front of their noses, blunting the horrible smells around them. No one bathed. Dental hygiene was basically unknown. Rubbish littered the streets as sewage flowed past. Even though everyone was accustomed to this highly aromatic life, still some of the smells were hard to take. By floating your own favourite scent before your nose you might be able to forget that the person next to you smelled like a rotten piece of meat.

It all begins with the costume

Your meeting with the costume designer if you are doing a period play can teach you more about your character than hours analysing the script. Ask questions. What kind of undergarments would the character have worn? Can I feel the texture of the fabric? Why is it fastened like that? And so on. If you are doing a scene study class or a class in style, *your first decision is what costume you might wear.* (You can either go through the pages of costume design texts covering that period or go online and look at drawings of the period.)

Once you have an idea of what you might wear, find something to rehearse in that will give you some of the *same physical feedback.* Think about it. Your clothing gives you all kinds of feedback. If you are wearing trainers and jeans, you sit, sprawl, curl up on the floor, legs akimbo. Women, if you are wearing stiletto heels and a tightly-fitting short skirt, could you move and sit in the same ways? Men, in a three-piece elegant suit and solid leather shoes, how differently would you move?

Our clothing gives us permission to make or prevents us from making all kinds of movements that we generally don't even think about. Until women began wearing trousers they would never have dreamed of walking or sitting in the casual ways we've grown accustomed to. An anorak gives the body a very different message than a cape. One notices that Shakespeare played in modern dress often illuminates the text. I believe that's because we see the actors behaving naturally in a way that is easier to relate to, as the clothing and physicality reflects our own.

Now, let's move our minds back to the eighteenth century: men in two-inch heels wearing silk britches with special fastenings around the groin *just begging to be shown off.* Wouldn't it feel quite natural for you to move your leg into a slight 'turn out' to show just how well endowed you are and how the expensive silk highlights this fact?

Women not only fainted because their corsets were so tight they couldn't breathe, but those corsets demanded a posture and a certain style of 'reclining while sitting'. To sit as we sit today would have been very uncomfortable. Suddenly, just feeling in your body what that stricture would be like, you long to stretch your arm to rest it on the back of the settee and lean sideways so you have more room to breathe. You also find yourself tilting your head coquettishly to the opposite side – to keep your balance. The jump into Lydia Languish (*The Rivals)* is not hard at all.

Once again, I am encouraging you to **let your body guide you instead of your head**. I believe shoes are the most important piece of clothing for an actor *because they determine how you will walk as the character*. Haunt charity shops and find yourself shoes and boots that can serve you for auditions and rehearsals for many period pieces. Women, two- to three-inch heels – no higher – 'character shoes'. Men, a boot or shoe with a firm sole and hopefully a little heel. Practise your monologues in those shoes. Notice how your posture might change and your steps become firmer.

Period language: What does that mean?

Once you accept that this thing called 'style' is achieved through your sensitivity to the character's clothing (or an approximation of it) you can then turn your attention to other challenges lurking in period plays. The first thing that strikes all of us when working on seventeenth- and eighteenth-century plays is the language. Wow! The language can be convoluted, extravagant and nothing like anything that has ever come out of our own mouths. However, once we get well into the nineteenth and twentieth centuries it becomes much easier. The television series, *Downton Abbey*, has exquisite detail in period costumes and sets, but the language is not that distant at all.

This is where you want your Intellect to be quiet so you can trust your intelligence (prefrontal cortex) to figure out what your character is actually saying, without your Intellect telling you how hard this is or that you can't possibly 'relate to it'. Just as with Shakespeare, where we must *translate terms no longer in use*, we must do the same with Restoration comedy and other high-style works. Expressions that were hilarious 300 years ago might mean nothing to us now. With a good glossary, once you understand what you are saying, you will be amazed at how clear it will suddenly become – and then clear to your audience as well.

The next hurdle is for you to trust that *once you understand the meaning, your brain makes all the connections you need*. It will reference those words and expressions against your entire vocabulary and your life experiences. **That is why when you work with your Dungeon open you can be surprised that an antiquated term – a phrase or word you have never used previously in your life – will resonate within you.**

That is when the fun begins. I don't believe it serves theatre, art or entertainment to offer up period plays like museum pieces. I'm clearly not in the minority as I see Nicholas Hytner at the National Theatre in

London, among others, direct many of these kinds of plays, breathing so much fresh vitality into them that we are amazed we ever thought them dreary or difficult.

Connecting to the text

Once your body is moving as the character, *getting cues from the costume*, and you have a clear understanding of your text, you now have the opportunity to let those words explore feelings. (Of course you will *tune* yourself and approach this work with your wide open Dungeon!) Do not for a moment think that just because your character speaks in rhymed couplets or uses bizarre expressions he or she is in some way emotionally stunted. Making the assumption that your character feels a limited range of emotions can only lead you to the kind of exaggerated, gimmicky acting we associate with badly-done period comedy: funny faces, funny voices and funny walks.

Not long ago I was teaching a comedy class where one of the actors decided to tackle Lady Wishfort from *The Way of the World* (Congreve, 1700.) A lady of a 'certain age', she is the butt of humour as she seeks a romantic liaison. The playwright and the other characters clearly find this laughable. She has long speeches where she rails against rejection and stupidity as she plots to entice and seduce.

The trap of this character is to play her as an angry clown where she simply becomes tiresome and not very funny. The actor in my class, with a trusty handkerchief in hand, a shawl (over her T-shirt) wrapped around her middle so tightly her breasts perched above it precariously (to simulate the corset) and shoes she purposely chose to be a little too tight (she wore double socks with them) launched into one of Lady Wishfort's speeches with phrases like: 'Frippery! Superannuated frippery!' and 'I shall die with confusion if I am forced to advance . . . but I shall not be too coy neither.' With Dungeon wide open, her Lady Wishfort seemed to *embody her name*. Oh, how she *wished* for *it*. Her longing, her fears, her uncertainty and her blatant sexual hunger careened through the text. With her emotions on cue, she was in tears one moment, giggling like a teenager the next and moving her shoulders seductively the next. We, in the audience, were gasping for air, we were all laughing so hard. And the most remarkable thing is that as we found her hilarious, we also found her touching as we saw real needs and real frustrations.

There is, of course, one more element in acting in any of the classics: your voice. You'll recall that I have urged you to find a good vocal warm-up you can do practically every day to keep your voice healthy and strong. If you are doing mostly film and television, there are not great demands made on your voice. In fact, you must learn to keep the level quite low, still maintaining intensity and energy – a very important skill in itself, but *not a good choice for acting the classics*.

Once you begin to deal with texts like Restoration comedy, Molière, Racine, Shakespeare, Shaw, you immediately encounter vocal challenges. *You also notice that articulation needs to be sharper as you work with playwrights who utilize alliteration and repetition of words or phrases for special impact*. You realize very quickly that we have all become incredibly lazy in our normal pronunciation.

Therefore, your basic care of your instrument should keep your voice supple and your articulators sharp. Assuming you are in prime vocal condition, *you can embrace the inherent music within the text*. What do I mean by that? Every writer uses language in their own way. Think about the rhythms and word choice David Mamet uses typically. How incredibly different that is than Tennessee Williams or Oscar Wilde? It's not just a matter of the time periods when they wrote, but the unique rhythmic quality of their lines.

In musical terms, Williams loves *legato*, his characters repeating a phrase sometimes three or four times – usually including long vowel sounds. Mamet adores *staccato*. His characters often speak with the rapid fire of a machine gun, short, sharp words with hard-hitting consonants.

Sometimes you will be fortunate enough to have a teacher or director work with you and the text in this way. But if you are on your own, taking on the challenges of classics where you must fulfil the musical demands of the text, I want you to begin to listen and then to think *musically*.

Look at Lady Wishfort's line, 'Frippery. Superannuated frippery'. If you mumble those gorgeous consonants and fail to savour the power in the repetition of that word, 'frippery', you will not understand the character. Unlike naturalistic theatre, you're not trying to find a way to make her 'like someone you have known before'. She's a unique creation: larger, greedier, sillier than most people would ever dare to reveal. That's what makes her so delicious for the audience.

But isn't all this *technical* work on the text contrary to being 'real' and in the moment? Absolutely NOT! **You are a consummate artist.** You can and should *do it all*. If the *only* thing you do is bite consonants and arc a line perfectly without any connection to your body, yes, you will be guilty of the same lifeless acting we've seen in bad productions of style plays.

But just as you are able to hit your mark on a film set, or make sure you are heard in the back of the theatre, you can make all kinds of 'technical' demands on yourself – remember that golfer? You can think of them as 'given circumstances' or simply as living up to the music you've been given. If you sing, you know that in a particular song, coming in on the third beat is not negotiable no matter how you feel emotionally. This whole chapter is really about that 'great balancing act'.

Try this little experiment if you don't believe me that you can do it all. Activate your pelvis, open your jaw and put your arms into the 'don't touch me' position. Say Lady Wishfort's line, 'Frippery. Superannuated frippery!' Push the air away with your hands and really bite into all those lovely consonants. Enjoy the flood of feelings. The muscles in your mouth, jaw and throat are being recruited and you can begin to *embody the outrage in those lines*. You will find if you try this several times, moving your body in different ways, that the line reading will change. If you rotate your pelvis you may find the character's 'wishing for it'! *Acting with passion* is not about setting a line reading – it's about the discoveries you can make when you combine all your technical expertise with an open Dungeon.

Creating a character who is unlike you

Every class I teach, as actors experience themselves freely connecting with emotions and their bodies feeling open and light, I ask a key question. What about characters who can't express their feelings easily?

This is obviously a *very important question*. Not every character has a beautifully aligned body. Not every character is 'in touch with their feelings'. The range from uptight and withheld to free and open is enormous. Your job is to *explore this range*. And what fun it is!

My general advice in character creation is pretty straightforward:

- Pay attention to what your playwright says in description.

- Notice what other characters say or how they respond to your character.

- Pay attention to the given circumstances that have shaped the character.

- Pay attention to the character's own words – especially when they talk about themselves. Be warned, **characters often lie, or are deluded about themselves**, so take most of their opinions with a grain of salt (you'll notice I did not suggest creating the character's previous history out of your imagination or any form of backstory; I want you to stick to the facts).

While you are absorbing the storyline, actions, relationships in a play, your *intelligence is seeking the nuanced facts* pertaining to your character in the script, as you read, reread and memorize. Excellent. **The challenge is keeping your Intellect from getting busy trying to tell you how to *act* all of it.** Once again, I want you to trust your incredible brain's intuitions and your body. Processing all the information available within the text can set in motion the building of your sense of this character.

You're going to let your body be your guide. As you experience an 'uptight character', for example, you will actually begin to feel your body tense in response. *You will be creating the character's armour.* Let me walk you through this. You will, in fact, be *reconstructing* some of the muscular tension you've just worked so hard to get rid of. However, you will be doing this as a *choice*. These tensions are not your *definition* or *limitation* as an actor any longer. You can, at will, however, let any character *borrow* them.

As you begin to shut down any movement in your pelvis – in response to your character's fear of anger, you'll start to feel all the peripheral muscles being recruited. Your knees may begin to lock, your thighs feel more rigid. You might notice that just by doing that, the muscles around your mouth will feel more rigid. Your lips may purse. Your character tries to smile to cover those darker feelings and you notice a rigidity in your mouth and cheeks. You are experiencing the knock-on effect in the creation of armour. **You sense how much it *costs* this character to be so under control.**

You begin to actually *feel* like the character. Because this is such a different way to go about building a character – so many schools of thought would have you *thinking* about the character's childhood formative events, or having you relate to things in your own life – you are going to feel, once again, as though you are balancing on a tightrope without a safety net. **But you are building that character truly from the inside.** So keep balancing. It's not life-threatening. Be curious. Experiment. Try not to 'set' things, but *trust your body to guide you*.

'Dying is easy, comedy is hard'

That often-quoted line is attributed to many famous actors of comedy, and certainly resonates with all of us. It is a cruel tyranny to make an audience laugh night after night – and an unbelievable joy when it happens.

There's very little funnier than watching people suffer – comedy and tragedy are divided by a paper-thin wall of context. *Comedy is at its core about people dealing with situations that become increasingly difficult* – usually of their own making. (French farce, where a seemingly harmless dishonest act at the beginning of the play pushes the leading character to lie upon lie, forcing the character, ultimately, to increasingly desperate lengths to prevent discovery.) We watch characters struggle, rush around trying to fix things, hiding and being desperately uncomfortable. **Watching people being happy is not funny.**

Charlie Chaplin's little tramp character was beloved by audiences as they watched him face one miserable situation after another. His never giving up no matter how impossible the odds made it funny. Had he been beaten down by these situations (and how easy that would have been) it would have made us cry.

When actors are first exposed to *acting with passion* they think it's their key *only to playing tragedy* – the more serious the better. It isn't until they approach comedy in exactly the same way – open Dungeon, emotions fully available – that they realize how much easier it is to do comedy in this way, rather than *trying* to be funny. Quite often an actor will work on a monologue where previously he's loaded it with clever line readings, gimmicks and tricks that do provoke *some* laughter. However, by letting the text take him into the character's real anger and frustration, it becomes effortlessly hilarious. Directors often advise their cast to play the comedy seriously, but it's hard for actors to understand this until they experience it. Until then, it just seems counterintuitive.

Back to our French farce, those brilliant plays of Georges Feydeau: we watch the leading man having to hide the woman he's about to seduce, while trying to put on a beard so as to fool his wife into thinking he is someone else. The more desperately and seriously he attempts these subterfuges, the funnier. When he sees a lacy undergarment on the bed just before opening the door for his wife, his genuine horror is hilarious. As he stuffs the frilly knickers into his breast pocket we delight in his narrow escape and look forward to his using the knickers to wipe his brow.

I challenge you to memorize a comedy monologue. Then try doing it with the same commitment you would give to Greek tragedy and see what happens.

Timing: It's true. Comedy is all about timing

Just as you were thinking, *so that's all there is to it*, I'm going to present you with another challenge. Comedy is fragile. If the audience *has time to think about the absurdity being presented*, if the pace slows down and they can anticipate that something is *supposed* to be funny, there is no surprise. Hence, no laughter. This suspension of disbelief seems to be *bound up with rhythm* – and generally, the rhythms of comedy are quick.

In previous generations, when actors learned their craft through apprenticeship in acting companies, they learned timing by watching and listening to the successful actors around them. They imbibed the quick pace of the comedies presented. They knew they must meet the demands of the quick pace set by director and cast. They needed to figure out how to 'land a line' and 'bite a cue'. Being slow to pick up a cue could mean humiliating criticism. These skills – thought of as *technique* and therefore looked down upon by some actors – **I want you to excel at them**.

I learned an invaluable lesson early in my acting career that has served me in every comedy I have ever directed. I was incredibly lucky and was cast in a wonderful supporting role in my first Broadway play. The character was quite funny and I'd been very well directed to the point where I had one line that would bring *such a big laugh that it turned into a round of applause each night*. In fact, *The New York Times* review talked about that laugh – that's how big it was.

We were in around the third month of our run when, one evening, as I was doing the scene and said 'the line', there was only scattered, muted laughter. Well, of course, I left the stage saying, 'What a terrible audience.' But then, the next night it was the same, and the next. *At the end of a week I was suicidal. I had no idea what had happened.* I thought I was saying the line in the same way, same intention, same commitment. The stage manager had no idea and our director was far away.

In our cast was an elderly grande dame of the theatre. She'd played Gertrude to Barrymore's Hamlet! She adored the young actors in the company. So I went to her dressing room. She immediately said, 'You've lost *the laugh*.' I asked if she would watch the scene to see if she could tell me what I was doing wrong. She stood in the wings that performance and afterwards, when I came offstage – naturally no laugh – she said, **'You took a breath before you said the line.'** Next performance, **I took my breath *before the cue line was completed* – *biting the cue*** – and, yes, huge laugh, round of applause. In taking the nanosecond long breath before I spoke, I had broken the rhythm and signalled to the audience 'this is going to be funny', thus killing any laughter.

How does an actor develop that crucial sense of timing? Your first step is awareness. The second is *commitment to the discipline needed to be open and in the moment*, **at the same time you are living up to the rhythmic/technical demands**. (Like being a singer!) You'll notice that in almost every comedy much of the dialogue is composed of short, quick lines. You don't see as many long speeches as in more introspective plays. The characters interact, often interrupting each other, or saying only a word or two in response. These rapid-fire dialogues are wonderful for you to practise the skill of biting cues.

Think about your conversations with close friends. How often do you interrupt each other? How often do you finish each other's sentences? You and a friend are recounting a funny incident. You each keep adding in more detail with every line of the exchange. If you were to record the conversation, you would probably not hear any pauses at all. Put your antennae on alert for this and *notice how seldom we have long 'meaningful' pauses* in conversations and arguments. Even though actors adore them.

What has happened in your easy-going conversation or disagreement is that you and your friend were each *so eager to talk* that you didn't let *a whisper of air go in between the words you spoke to each other*. That's what it means to 'bite cues'.

Your challenge is to do this onstage. That means you must learn to **take a breath on the last two or three words of your cue line, *not at the end of the cue***. It's the only way you can come in seamlessly with your line. Look at this two-line exchange:

A: It's a long life.
B: Not if you keep eating my chips.

The words ' life' and 'Not' should be glued together as though they are one sentence. Then you begin to sense the underlying rhythmic structure of comedy dialogue. I believe this structure *supports the actor just as a good band will support a singer*.

Once you have explored this technique you'll be surprised that it starts to be quite easy. *That's because you've been doing it all your life unconsciously.* Think about it. Have you *ever* run out of breath at the end of a sentence when you were in a conversation? And, how common is it that we find ourselves jumping in to say something when we argue or get excited? Breathing (luckily) is handled by our autonomic nervous system. Which means we don't have to think about it.

We actually take in a breath on the *impulse* to say something and that might be in the middle of our friend's sentence, since by then we've arrived at the point being made and are anxious to respond. *That's exactly what I'm asking you to do when you bite cues*. Once again, I want you to mirror life rather than do an artificial version of it.

Now, the next step is to *land the line*. **One of the ways some actors try to assure themselves they won't be overacting, or appearing less than natural, is to do a lot of *throwing away* of lines.** They learn to mumble some of the words – usually the final words in the line. This letting the words trail off has an *effortless* feel to it. 'Look at my not pushing at all. Oh, how *real* I must seem.' This works to some extent with some characters and at times for film or television. But for comedy onstage it can be a disaster. (Unless this is built into the underlying humour of the character.)

We must go back to the *music of the text*. The two-line exchange above. If the word 'chips' trails off and can't be heard by the audience, there's no chance it will get a laugh. If the word 'chips' is *lifted and 'landed'* and the situation and characters support it, it will be funny. This doesn't mean that it's louder or highly inflected. It just means that the word *means something to you*, the actor, and to your character, and therefore cannot be discarded.

Quite often when I'm giving notes as a director, I'll find myself saying, 'I couldn't hear that final word.' All the actors have to do is remind themselves to head towards the ends of those sentences with energy and the whole scene will take off and soar. Now, read this five-line exchange from a very funny play by Tony Sportiello called, *Star Power*. The director and producer are considering a film star for the lead in their next fringe production.

Director: He can't act.
Producer: He can so act!
Director: He can't.
Producer: Well, he can act enough.
Director: You didn't see those sequels.

Can you sense the rhythms? Read it aloud with a friend. Notice that 'He can act enough' could get a small laugh. If, however, *you bite the cue for the next line –* **suppressing that laugh** *– and head for the word 'sequels'*, you'll get a big laugh on the end of that line.

Which brings me to my final piece of advice. *Comedy is driven by energy*. It's like the magic fairy dust that makes every kind of acting – stage, film, television – shine. *It is often called charisma or star quality*. And certainly, when you see an actor who draws your attention, you sense there is some magnetic/energetic pull.

This has always sounded mysterious. Some actors have 'it' and others don't, *has been the assumption*. I believe we can turn that assumption on its head. **The biggest energy vampire is your Intellect telling you to be cautious.** I have seen actors emerge from behind their masks and fortresses and carefully crafted 'acts'. *They literally glow with energy*. For now, trust, when you open your Dungeon and say, **'Look at me. I want you to see me!' You can do it all – timing, style and unforgettable characters that make us laugh and cry.**

8

AUDITIONS: YOUR CHANCE TO SHINE

I remember years ago rushing to my therapist's office after an audition, feeling completely gutted. She smiled as she said, 'Ah, Niki, you only ever audition for *two people* all your life. Your mother and your father.' (For each of us, whoever was responsible for our safety and survival those early formative years, becomes our direct link to the limbic system and our fears of rejection.)

No wonder I would feel *overwhelming fear* and nerves as I walked into an audition. I could see that the *life and death terror* I felt at auditions was clearly a short circuit into my Dungeon. I was connecting with my pre-verbal feelings. If my parents had rejected me I would most certainly have died. So even though I could *logically* see that failing to win the love of these casting directors would not lead to instant death, I was still engulfed by surges of fear that defied logic. **On the positive side, once you understand the workings of this profound primitive response, *you can embrace it and utilize it to make every audition fully alive and exciting.*** Learning to truly shine at every single audition is an integral part of *acting with passion*.

Fear of failure

We can all agree that one of the main obstacles you face at a casting is the fear of failure. It sends you into your *fight or flight* mode and wreaks havoc with your desire to look professional and confident. You are now familiar with the feedback loop from body to brain and back again and the arsenal of defences your body puts into place as soon as *any danger* message is received. Your heart begins to pound violently. Your throat closes and your mouth can turn to sandpaper. You feel your stomach muscles clench.

With these surges of terror *the Intellect begins to scream*. Remember, this is not the wisdom of a loving coach. **It's your five-year-old self, feeling out of control.** Listen to the instructions from the Intellect:

- Oh, no! You are nervous again.
- You must get control of yourself!
- Stop all that trembling!
- Get a grip.
- They can *see* you are nervous!
- You'll look unprofessional!
- You will make a fool of yourself.
- You must push down all those feelings.
- Hide your nervousness.
- Now, put on that confident face.
- Big smile!

The mask you learned to put on when you were young is now firmly in place. No one can possibly see what you *really* feel. Your intellect is aided and abetted by some odd advice we all seem to have been given. Teachers telling you that you can learn 'not to take it personally' and that's the real definition of 'being a pro'. Somehow you should just 'give it your best shot, *but don't invest too much*'. This advice just doubles the volume of advice from the Intellect recommending all kinds of behaviours so as to *appear* as though you *don't care all that much*.

From the other side of the table

Having directed plays for many years, I have sat through countless auditions. My heart goes out to the actors because I know how hard it is. But even with all my compassion and first-hand knowledge, the realities of the audition process create many obstacles. The first is *time*. You end up *seeing too many actors* in the course of a day. You sit with your producer, your stage manager, possibly the playwright. Fatigue sets in.

My experience has been that there are many, many talented actors. Talent is not the issue. The problem is that sometimes it's quite difficult to really *see* the richness of the talent. Actors are so busy trying to *look professional and convince everyone that they are confident*. In the process they have listened to all that advice from the Intellect. Thus, they have stuffed down their fear in the only way available: with tension and wearing a mask. The body becomes tight. The trembling in the face disappears and the mask with a brittle smile takes its place. The voice doesn't shake, that's true, but it lacks vibrancy.

In walks the *professional* actor, who looks me squarely in the eyes, shakes my hand firmly and says, 'Hell of a play.' That means at the end of the day, when we auditors discuss the actors, we can hardly distinguish one from another. They all blend into each other because they all look alike. It's not that they give *bad* auditions, or stupid line readings. They're just all so masked and covered that it's hard to feel excited about them.

The biggest lesson I've learned is that at every audition, whether it's for a West End or Broadway play, a television commercial or a fringe musical, your audience of decision-makers is looking for one thing: **they are hoping that *life – vibrating, pulsing aliveness* – will walk in the door**.

Willingness to remove the mask and do it wrong

The sparkling eyes, the excitement that auditors sit up and notice is really just your *willingness to enter the room with your Dungeon wide open*. Actors work so hard and train so hard to *look professional – meaning not showing even a hint of fear*. It's odd that we have been made to think of this as the ideal. Your open Dungeon might mean your hands tremble and we can see that you are nervous – but the director would have to be incredibly stupid not to understand that *any actor who really cares would naturally be nervous*. Assuming you aren't auditioning for that one in a thousand, your excitement, your flushed face, your shaking hands, all communicate the *vitality the auditors are longing to see*.

Stories abound about stars whose 'discovery' came through an audacious or unconventional audition – basically doing it wrong. Some have, no doubt, been embellished, but the universal message in these theatre myths is: *dare to be uniquely yourself*.

One of the most famous stories is about Barbra Streisand. She had been singing in small clubs around New York earning next to nothing and unable to get an agent. Fortunately someone involved in the casting for a musical called *I Can Get it For You Wholesale* saw her act one night. They were desperate to cast the role of Miss Marmelstein. They'd seen many actors/singers. No one seemed right.

The producers and director finally agreed to see this *complete unknown*. Her audition time was set for 2.00 at the theatre. Sitting out front, the auditors waited. Two o'clock came. Two o'clock passed. Just at the point when they were ready to leave, outraged at being stood up, a young woman raced onto the stage. She was a mess. Her clothing, soon to be her trademark, was charity shop vintage, coat hanging open, hair dishevelled and wearing *two different shoes*.

She apologized in a flurry, explaining that she'd been held up. Seeing a bar stool on the stage, she pulled it to her. She dropped her coat in a puddle on the floor. Perched on the stool she then reached into her mouth for chewing gum that she proceeded to glue underneath the seat, without apology. She nodded to the pianist in the pit.

The rest is history. Except for the fact that the stage manager, so horrified that anyone would put chewing gum on a piece of stage furniture, checked the stool. There was no gum! Streisand broke all the rules. And she broke them on purpose. Was she terrified? You bet. According to her self-accounts she, like every performer, has her demons and her terrors. What she had learned from so much rejection and advice about 'fixing herself to be less ethnic, less odd' was to embrace her uniqueness and dare.

Auditions come in many different forms

Whether it's a theatre or a television commercial casting you always want to be sure your Dungeon is open and *you* are there shining through offering your broken heart, your joy and your passion.

You will go through your *self-tuning* before you leave your apartment for the day. Lucky you! If you feel frightened, your Dungeon is already cracked open. Please don't ever again be angry with yourself for the nerves that are natural when you're going to be 'judged'. Be delighted because *all of your emotions are ready to play*.

Once you've *tuned* yourself, you can go off and enjoy your day and be confident your body will be ready to receive the signals you will be giving it later on. Before your audition, simply nip into the bathroom and cue those connections. Within seconds you will revive the sense of your Dungeon opening and your body feeling alive with excitement. *Your fear will continue to make this even easier!* You can whisper the word 'fear' as you touch your broken heart and your stomach, and then permit your hands to reach out, making little fists and opening. A pelvic thrust and a big push away with your arms and you're ready to win!

That means that every audition you get, even if it's for something where you feel you are totally wrong for the part, *you will use it as an opportunity to explore auditioning this way*. My students tell me how much more fun they are having because for the first time the audition is for *them*. Whether they land the role or not, they know they've engaged fully and therefore *owned the experience*.

Each time you are in front of auditors it's a chance to show them *how good you are*. *My* hidden agenda, therefore, is that for every role for which you are *not* cast, **I hope the director is *tortured* throughout rehearsals.** The director was looking for a tall blonde and in you walk, dark and short, so you are rejected. But when that director has to work with the other actor who can't cut it, every night he will be kicking himself saying, 'I could have wigged that brunette. Why didn't I cast her? She was fantastic!' Yes, I want him to *suffer* and then *cast you the next time*. I can't tell you how many times my students tell me about successful casting that has come from a *previous* audition. It never hurts for people to *see how talented you are – then they remember you*.

Given that, however, as you all know, each type of audition is its own unique 'game'. I want you to be a champion at all of them. We'll start with theatre auditions.

The theatre casting

I think it's hard for actors, so gripped in their own fear of failure, to understand that *fear* is also raging on the other side of the table. The more money at stake in a production, the more fear. *Casting directors fear producers and directors*. If they fail to bring the 'right' actors they are in for abuse or being fired. Producers are sucking on their antacids thinking of all the money that could be lost and with it their list of 'satisfied investors'. Directors worry that without good actors the play will bomb and their reputation will be tarnished, and so on.

If you recall, *fear* makes it harder to think clearly. That means the auditors are not going to have *subtle perceptions*. They need to be practically hit on the head. Think of that Barbra Streisand story I related. They were unconsciously hoping to see something *electric to make them feel certain*. How do *you* create that electricity?

If you are auditioning for a fringe or an off-off Broadway show, the stakes financially are much lower. That doesn't mean the egos, the uncertainty and the anxiety among auditors do not exist. They, too, want to find the best actors for their play and they know that it's hard to perceive from an audition who is really going to deliver. Often for these auditions you might be given more time and even many call-backs as the people involved have less experience and therefore find it harder to make decisions.

Whether you will be standing on the stage of a large West End or Broadway theatre, in a rented rehearsal room or the tiny theatre upstairs at a pub, *there are many things over which you have control*.

Making choices

What do I mean by that? If you have been given a script and told what scenes will be read, don't read the play *trying to decide all the motivations and psychology* you can reveal about the character. In other words, don't begin by trying to decide how *to act this part* or, worse still, what any particular line reading should sound like. I'll share a secret: **there is no such thing as a *wrong* line reading at an audition**. The director, playwright, producer, are not seeking out your ability to give them a perfect script analysis. *They are hoping you can bring the script to life.*

Start memorizing! Now you know how to get your neurons firing. Depending upon how much time you have and how specific the script assignment is, you want to be comfortable with long speeches and the flow of quick dialogue so you don't find yourself trapped in the book. You also know that *the more familiar you are with the text, the more likely you will be to connect to the feelings in your Dungeon.*

With your memorization will also come ideas about who this character is. Your agent might tell you the brief description given to them. These are usually so generic that they are only marginally helpful: 'Max: an aggressive thirty-five-year old, who has experienced setbacks recently. Middle class'. Or, 'Stella: wanting to please, this sensitive twenty-something always gets it wrong'. Hmm? Or they tell you *which star* they would cast if they could and would you please be similar.

It's impossible to play 'an idea'. Remember, acting is a *physical activity* not a mental one. Your job is to make a *choice* about the character that permits you to bring a particular energy onto the stage. Let's take those two rather thin descriptions and play with them, assuming the character is not well developed and that's about all the insight you have to work with.

. For Max, you might make the decision that he's athletic and maybe because he's aggressive he works out at a gym, shadow boxing and using a punching bag. See what happens when you read some of his lines simply absorbing that choice. You might find yourself using gestures that have a sort of punch in them. You'll notice that the choice I described is *physical*. And that's the trick, not to be trapped by an *emotional idea* of a character, but instead to look for a physical expression. The 'middle class' piece of the description may offer you an idea about where his accent falls on the spectrum. You certainly don't want him to sound posh and aristocratic. This piece of information is also helpful to you in deciding what you will wear to the audition.

Yes, I'm suggesting you always make a clear decision about how you will *costume* yourself. Remember, the people looking at you are hoping one of the actors they see will *hit them over the head* with the idea: '*This actor is perfect for the role!*' Now, this doesn't mean if it's a period piece you run over to the costume shop of the nearest theatre and rent a full nineteenth-century morning coat and tails. Instead you will comb your own wardrobe, or a friend's, and wear something that gives a hint of that costume – a well-cut jacket and maybe a cravat. Most emphatically it means not wearing blue jeans and trainers.

While we are on the subject of trainers, here's a little 'Niki rant'. I want you to be comfortable and am delighted for you to wear whatever makes you feel like you can move easily. *But please be aware that shoes determine your walk.* They are the most important piece of any costume.

Back to Max. If the script tells you he's hanging out with friends at home, please wear you grungiest 'at home' clothing. You might even give him a couple of days without a shave. But if he's coming from a job interview and just arriving at his friend's flat, put him in a business suit and tie. (He's had setbacks, he wants to look his best.) Then you have the engaging movements of being able to take off your jacket and loosen your tie during the audition.

Do I believe I've guessed *exactly* the way the director has visualized Max? Absolutely not! My goal is not for you to try to become a mind-reader. No matter how the production team has envisioned the character you are giving them something memorable and engaging with *your* choice. The director can then ask you to read the scene a second time to more closely match her preconceived idea. I'll be talking to you later in the chapter about this crucial piece of auditions – responding to ideas from the director.

On the subject of 'costuming for auditions': if you are called back, *wear exactly what you wore to that first audition.* If you have six call-backs, *keep wearing it!* I've seen actors lose a chance at a role because they couldn't imagine they should wear the same clothing for a call-back. 'Where's that girl who wore the white dress? We liked her, didn't we?'

Now what about Stella? You hear the words 'sensitive and gets it wrong'. How tempting to begin working on how she *feels*. Instead, let's make some choices about how she moves and what she wears. Does she run in headlong and then stop herself up short with uncertainty? Is she angular in her movement rather than graceful? Does she go to yoga class but her head is so busy telling her she's doing it wrong that she keeps stopping herself to correct something? You might work on the script at home while making failed attempts at doing warrior poses. Or maybe work on the lines while trying to do ballet, often correcting yourself. You would begin to gain a sense of how she might move.

If she's insecure, you want to choose clothing to wear that would show that she has *tried* to get it right, but still something is *off*. I would suggest you don't wear your sexy high-heeled shoes unless you can walk in them *safely* as someone who *wants* to be sexy but finds those shoes *impossible* to walk in. A thought about those shoes you adore. Very few young women walk easily and comfortably in the super-high-heeled shoes so in fashion. They throw your weight off balance and *can force you to tighten your knees and your pelvis* – not really a formula for looking sexy at all. They also make a strong visual statement about the character. So, please do consider very carefully before wearing them for auditions.

To sum up, your preparation is active. Lying in bed worrying or trying to *imagine* how the auditors will respond is no help at all. Use the time wisely to at least get familiar enough with the script that you can read it with ease and hopefully have parts of it memorized so you can be completely free to connect with feelings. Even for so-called 'cold readings' you generally have a chance to look at the script beforehand. Spend that valuable time training your eye to *read the words fluently* rather than *making acting choices*. Reading the scene aloud purely to understand what is happening permits your unconscious to listen.

Monologues

There was a time when doing a prepared monologue for an audition was pretty standard everywhere. In New York you will still find auditions where you will be asked to do a monologue, especially for some casting directors and agents – in London and Paris this rarely happens. On both sides of the Pond you will be asked to come prepared with two or three monologues to gain entrance to a drama school or to audition for a theatre company like the RSC or the National Theatre in London.

Do I believe you should have several monologues *well-memorized and ready to go just in case?* Yes! Absolutely. I often get urgent emails from actors needing monologue suggestions because a director or agent has asked for one. Don't wait till you are under the gun. An opportunity like that does not come along often. Why take the chance of being *underprepared* by having to suddenly decide on something to memorize?

Because I hope you will be working the muscles in your brain by trying to learn a new piece every week, you will already be ahead of the game. However, some of those monologues will be purely for your own growth and pleasure and not necessarily your best audition choices. How do you choose strong audition monologues?

- A role you could be cast in: the right age, close in type.

- Not the 'flavour of the month': the monologue everyone is doing.

- Keep it short: never longer than two minutes (time it to be sure).

- The basics: a classical piece, a modern piece, one funny, one serious.

- Surprise us: casting that isn't obvious but oh, so interesting once we see it.

- Something you enjoy doing: you must really love these pieces so you can have pleasure doing them no matter what the outcome of the audition.

- **Do not choose *dialogue* that you piece together**, requiring you to respond to words the auditors cannot hear.

An actor I'd trained asked for advice in choosing audition pieces for a Shakespeare theatre in the States. He was a natural Petruchio or Henry V – brawny and handsome. However, he knew he could only do two pieces and his competition was stiff. Fortunately I knew his work and urged him to highlight his range rather than showing his most obvious casting. He needed to be *memorable*. He knew he had to stand out against hundreds of actors.

The two monologues that landed him a place in the company were roles he *could* play, but were certainly *not obvious* for him. He chose a piece of Richard II where he could highlight his ability to flare with anger and strength – *but then reveal his vulnerability as well*. For comedy he did the heartbreak speech of Thisbe when she thinks Pyramus is dead at the end of *A Midsummer Night's Dream*. He played this with utter commitment and seriousness (remember, watching people suffer is funny). He let his tears flow and it was hilarious. They were bold choices.

Don't be surprised that making these kinds of decisions can be *very challenging*. You are looking for contrasts. You want to show as much range as possible, yet staying realistically within your casting – don't audition with a grandmother speech if you are twenty-five. This is another reason to become a memorizing machine – devouring interesting pieces so you have many to choose from. Show them to friends, ask them for their 'first impression'. That will tell you a great deal about how the auditors will see you.

Once you have chosen your monologues (and I believe you should have a couple of extra ones in case they ask for more), you want to practise them with some movement. Remember the chapter on gesturing? Go back to that chapter and remind yourself about how you want to *decide ahead of time where to place the various things you will reference in the text*. You are doing Lady Anne from *Richard III*. Where are the soldiers standing? Where is the coffin? Where does Richard enter from? *This gives your arms ample opportunity to reach out into space to address these various people and places.*

Another question you must decide on is where you will place your gaze. As we all know, **you cannot look at auditors directly**. They want to be able to observe you, take notes, sip coffee and not feel required to give you any feedback. But, you want them to *feel the intensity of your gaze.* Practising where to look for auditions is a great thing to do with your group of fellow actors.

How do you find the right place to look? Once you have entered the room or theatre you *immediately gauge the auditors' eye level*. You will then place the character to whom you are speaking *around that eye level – maybe a shade higher* depending upon the space. (In a theatre where the audience is sitting in a rake you usually want to place your eye level on the row directly behind the auditors' eyes.) Too many actors place the character they are addressing at such a bizarrely high level it looks like they are talking to a giant, or an angel floating in the sky.

You know from my advice on *trying to visualize* that I only want you to *see* and look at the chair next to the auditor or the back of the room, or the exit sign in the theatre – wherever you've decided to focus your eyes. 'Hello chair,' you are saying to yourself. Then, with Dungeon open you can fall in love, storm with rage or be heartbroken, seeing that chair or whatever else is *really* there.

Crucial: You begin your audition the *second* they can see you

Almost every experienced director will admit that they decide whether or not an actor is *right* for a part within *the first thirty seconds or less of the audition*. And that audition begins the second they see you. How you tiptoe into the room, or stride across the stage, gives an almost indelible sense of how you might play a role. Unfortunately, many actors seem to believe that they are *invisible* until they get 'into position' centre stage. That means they've *wasted or even undermined* that most valuable first impression.

Let's go back to the mind-set of the director: fatigued, frustrated, worried the right actor may never appear. In you walk. Your Dungeon is wide open. This means your eyes are sparkling, your cheeks might be trembling and flushed and your body is fully engaged. Don't be afraid it will be 'over the top'. You've chosen clothing that gives a sense of the character. That immediate gut-feel impression is, 'This might be the one!'

There's usually a moment or two of chit-chat. The auditor glances at your CV for the first time and notices you worked with Bert Jones. 'How was that?' they might ask. The questions aren't really to find out information. *The auditors want to see how you respond.* You are *auditioning in the way you laugh or don't laugh*; the way you say, 'Bert is a trip!' Are you standing with your body open and alive? Might you actually be showing some nervousness – I think that's great. It means you aren't hiding.

I will warn you that you are fighting all the years of being instructed on demonstrating your 'party manners' at first meeting someone. These lessons are deeply ingrained. 'I must be polite and pleasant.' Then the actor suddenly must shift into that other mode of 'actor'. Sadly, it may be too late. The impression is already made. 'No, that actor is simply too bland for the role.' Your *party manners* have already sealed the decision.

A real 'no guts no glory' approach to this entire first impression and chit-chat is to do it all *ever so slightly* as you think the character would. Let's go back to Max and Stella. You've been working on Max's lines while shadow boxing and can feel the drive and energy in your body and voice. Are you doing yourself a favour to walk onstage *less energized just because you normally do?* Well, the auditors do get to see you 'transform' yourself into Max in that case. But *maybe it's better* for them to think, 'Wow, we've found Max.' You decide.

With Stella it might be even trickier. Do you want them to think you, the actor, lack confidence? But, by the same token, you can give *the hint of her*, maybe dropping your bag as you enter, and laughing as you say, 'I can't get this bag to behave.' When you *smile in that slightly self-deprecating way you reveal immediately how fragile and sensitive you are*. I suggest you play with this approach. Possibly try it out for the first time for a play you aren't passionate about. See how it goes. Your Intellect will hate it, I promise. But auditors generally love it. Remember the Barbra Streisand story? The 'kookie' entrance she made was spot on for the character.

The reading

If you have been given the script in advance, you've become familiar enough with it that you can lift your eyes from time to time so the auditors *can really see your face*. Hold the script in your *upstage hand*. If you are reading with a stage manager, please don't upstage yourself! What I mean is, make sure you are standing *upstage of the other reader* where *they* have their back to the auditors and *you are facing the audience* and still able to make eye contact with the other reader. Too many actors head back into an acting class habit where they position themselves facing the scene partner directly and all anyone sees is their profile.

Holding the script, don't forget to let your armpits breathe! It's very easy to pull the script in tight to your body because of all the fear that is raging inside you. Remember the feedback loop. If you get your arms away from body centre the brain will ease off of its survival tactics. The hand holding the script can gesture a little, but mainly it is *your downstage arm that is free to talk*. It's also free to touch your body, your clothing, your throat and face. You can run your fingers through your hair. Every one of these gestures will not only help you to stay more connected, they will look natural and interesting. You won't look rigid or dull. If you lose your place or stumble over words, that's fine. *You're not being tested for your skill at reading.* The entire experience is only about how alive, engaging, emotionally open and energized you are. If you stumble on a word, you can say, 'Can I go back and do that again?' You can do this in an on-camera audition as well.

If you are dyslexic or have some other reading issue, make sure you get to the audition early so you can have *extra time with the script* if you don't get it in advance. For you, going over the lines aloud, slowly first and then speeding up, will be invaluable. Don't be afraid to mark your script with any help you might want – key words, breathing. Some actors scan a scene on their computer and then *copy it into a very large font* so it's easier to read under the stress of an audition. You also want to *learn to keep your thumb moving* down the page to mark where you are in the script at all times. That way you don't have to be worried that if you look up so your face can be seen, you will lose your place. I've worked with countless dyslexic actors who have made brilliant careers and have become quite skilled at readings.

'Now I'd like you to try it this way . . .'

Often actors groan inside when the director asks them to read a second time or do a memorized speech in a different way. *Instead you should be cheering.* **Directors will seldom choose to take time to work with an actor they haven't found interesting.** Your reading might, in fact, be perfect. The director wants to see how flexible you are, if you are an actor who 'takes direction' or sets a performance and can only do it one way. Or your reading is *close* to what the director is looking for but needs *a slight adjustment*.

Finally, you've come to the casting having made a bold set of choices about your Max or Stella. However, your agent got it all wrong. The character is entirely different. But you are clearly talented and appealing. The director wants to see if you can make a real 180-degree turn and find the true character. There are many different reasons for a director asking you to try it again – *all of them mean you are auditioning well*.

Directors never ask you to read a second time if they don't think you are interesting enough to consider.

The most important thing for you is to stay in your body! It's quite seductive for the Intellect to start telling you how to make these changes and how *pathetically wrong* your previous choices must have been. The second thing you must try to do is to *listen* to what the director is saying, seeking out *actions* rather than *feelings*. She says, 'I want you to be more upset when you don't get the prize.' It is so easy to begin to push emotions and think, 'Should I be crying or screaming?' Instead, let your character *want* that prize more – opening yourself to your deeply-held wants by opening your chest and letting your hands reach out or grasp. And then, just *let the feelings arise, whatever they are*.

Some directors will give you *confusing instructions* because they, themselves, are vague as to what they are really looking for. In this case, I would suggest you simply give yourself permission *to let go* even more. **The most typical danger in any audition is *playing it safe*.** The director can always ask you to do 'less'. That's a cue for you to *give your character the need to cover and hold back feelings* when they risk getting out of control. But, please permit yourself to be exciting, rather than *sensible*.

Television and film, take one

Casting for a great deal of television and film means you stand in front of a camera and give two or three takes of a short piece of memorized script. You might meet the casting director or you might not. *You will be judged solely upon what the camera has captured.* The decision-makers will be watching a great number of these takes. How do you make them sit up and take notice of you?

As you've gone through *acting with passion* you've experienced the excitement of knowing how to open your Dungeon to be fully present. **There is nothing the camera likes more than the effortless aliveness that you now can produce on cue.** I want you to *trust this.*

Actors are constantly being told that camera acting means 'doing less'. That's nonsense and leads actors to look stiff and flat because they are so busy *trying not to do too much*. It isn't that the camera needs you to 'contract' your normal acting. What the camera hates is bad acting!

Forced emotions, big facial expressions, wiggling eyebrows, look absurd on film. If you've worked in a group *self-tuning* and doing memorized pieces you will have noticed that actors' faces are incredibly open and clear when feelings are true and deep. You can see that, even with Shakespeare or Greek drama, the big feelings would translate perfectly to film because the actor is not 'making faces' but simply feeling.

This means you are well-prepared for the first hurdle in this kind of audition. You *will look alive and your acting will be seamless*. How you use your eyes for the camera is quite important. This is really technical, like learning to hit your mark to walk into a shot. Usually you will be told where to focus your eyes. It can be a little piece of paper stuck to the side of the lens or you may be looking directly into the lens itself. *Respect this instruction rather than feeling as though it is a limitation* on your ability to go with an impulse. (It's your 'given circumstance.')

Remember when I talked to you about the trap of *visualization*? The visual cortex is so rich in complexity *the less we layer it with instructions the better*. This means that if you've been told to look at the little yellow 'post-it note' attached to the camera and *imagine the face* of the love of your life, **ignore that instruction. Just look at the post-it note and *see* it**. *Don't try to visualize someone's face* superimposed on it. All that will happen is that you will shut off your Dungeon and you and your Intellect will be trying to control your visual cortex. All the camera will capture is effort.

It's actually ridiculously simple. *You see the post-it note and then let the words of the script* or the description of what you are supposedly seeing speak directly to the feelings inside you. You will be amazed at how completely you can fall in love with a tiny square of yellow paper!

It's quite tempting to show a change of thought by letting your eyes shift away from your focus point. The problem is that with a close-up *that small shift looks enormous*. If you feel the urge to look away, make it a teeny tiny movement only. If it's a long speech you might look down or up (ever so slightly) as we naturally do when thinking of what to say. But be very careful not to do this more than once in a short audition. When repeated *it can look artificial or a bad habit*. In fact, when you are learning the script at home, focus on one small spot to speak the words once they are memorized. If you can videotape yourself, you will see how sometimes a small movement will look natural and alive, but done three times it looks like bad acting.

Now, what do you do when they want 'alternate takes'? Like a theatre audition they are seeing how flexible you are. Mainly, however, they are hoping one of the takes will be perfection. Actors often get frustrated trying to figure out a way to make each take 'wildly different'. I recommend you look at this as a chance to be *curious* about who wants to come out of the Dungeon to play. With each take permit new feelings to bubble up without judgement. Take an open-throated breath between takes, touch your broken heart (possibly flex your hands in and out), stroke your cheek or neck for a moment, and then see where it takes you.

Hands in frame? You now know how important it is to let your hands speak as they do in life. **Do not underestimate how good this looks on camera.** With these filmed auditions the camera is usually in a medium close-up, meaning that we see to the middle of your chest. Having your hands hanging obediently at your sides *makes it visually less appealing to watch you*.

A trick I learned from a very clever camera operator was to let one hand come up into frame, touching your hair or your chin *as you take a breath* **before you speak the first words**. It makes you look more alive, as though you are *thinking before you speak*. Allow your hand to fall out of frame but then let it or even both hands come back into frame for a line or two as you continue. Raking your fingers through your hair looks great, touching your mouth for a moment if you feel emotions welling up gives us a sense of the character trying to stay in control. Experiment with a friend taking turns videotaping each other and see for yourselves. Since many of the actors competing against you will probably keep their hands obediently glued to their sides, you will have found a simple way of *making your film more distinctive*. And the more alive and natural you look, the better.

The interview for TV and film: 'Tell me what you've been doing'

If the production has a good-sized budget you will usually be seen in person by a casting director first. The casting director wants to see you at your best because then she's more likely to offer good candidates to the director and producer.

Casting directors believe the answer is to see the *real* you and hope it matches the character. In pursuit of that and the *myth* that you will *be more relaxed* if you 'chat' before you read the script, the casting director will ask you some general question about your career to get you talking. *Nothing is more uncomfortable for most actors than this false social exchange.* If you try to answer by talking about your most recent jobs or workshops you've taken, you know in your heart that it sounds hollow. You feel like a pathetic failure trying to brag about things you are sure the casting director couldn't be impressed with.

The whole exercise seems to me to be rigged to make the actor far *more* nervous, not less. For years as an actor I struggled with this, always feeling it must be *my fault* that I dreaded it and couldn't wait to finally *do the audition*. I hated it so much that now and then I would say, 'I'd really love to read *first* and then talk afterwards if that's okay.' No one ever said no, and that was an improvement.

But then I had an epiphany. I was talking to a friend of mine who had appeared on an evening talk show to publicize the new film she was starring in. I told her how funny and terrific she was. She said, 'I can't believe it. I was throwing up in the bathroom terrified I'd forget all the latest rewrites on that story I told.' I said, 'I beg your pardon?' She said, 'Oh, yes, we hired a writer, but then my manager, my agent and my coach all worked on it with me. We were changing things up till that afternoon. I was a mess.' She explained that every star interviewed has the same kind of extensive preparation for the *spontaneous clever stories* they relate. That thought marinated in my mind – but I didn't quite know what to do with it.

It happened that the following weekend I'd invited friends to my apartment for a dinner. I was going to make something fabulous: roast duckling. And because the group was large I put two ducks in my little basic oven. As we were enjoying our hors d'oeuvres suddenly the whole apartment filled with smoke. I heard sirens and within minutes a fireman had a ladder up to my third-floor window and was crawling through to save us all.

The following Monday afternoon I had an audition for a comedy film. When the casting director asked me, 'What have you been doing?' I blurted out the story of the disastrous dinner party I'd had over the weekend when I'd set my kitchen on fire. She laughed delightedly. She handed me the script, and hardly letting me finish my reading, said, 'Yes, you are perfect for this.'

The pieces fell into place. **I told that same story *for years* at countless auditions**, always beginning it with, 'I nearly burned down my apartment building last weekend.' Let's take a look at why this story of mine landed me many jobs.

When I teach this concept I ask the actors first to role-play the typical chit-chat interview. They recite credits from their CV and try to sound enthused about a recent short film or fringe show. We observe the actors looking self-conscious even as they try to act relaxed and friendly. Their faces look serious. Their hands remain politely in their laps. The Intellect is quick to remind them, 'It's bad manners to brag.' Then I ask them to tell a funny story of some experience they've had. The transformation is remarkable. Suddenly we see personality that is engaging and appealing. Their hands move in space *describing the event*. The actors look alive and spontaneous. Nothing is more appealing than seeing someone laugh at their own mistakes and foibles. *Exactly what most casting people are hungry to see at auditions.*

Bottom line. The funny story immediately makes you someone who stands out from the crowd and is more 'castable'. Just keep in mind:

- The best stories are ones where you've been embarrassed or made a fool of yourself.
- Stories about pets can be hilarious.
- Stories about cooking or party disasters are good.
- A recent vacation/holiday madness equally so.
- Stories about your children only work sometimes – if they are casting a mum or dad. Otherwise, if the casting director doesn't have children they might not relate.
- It's always best if you can laugh at yourself.
- Keep it short (that's why you rehearse it): under two minutes.

Is your Intellect going wild telling you how outrageous this sounds? Please, *try this out with some friends or fellow actors*. As you watch each other it will be very clear. You can even ask someone to run a video so you can judge for yourself. Watch both versions. First try being your 'likeable self' as you recite your recent accomplishments and then try the second version. You decide. Which do you think will be more helpful to your career?

The alternate universe of the commercial audition

More than any other kinds of casting, commercials are their own unique game. I want you to be good at the game because I want you to earn lots of money with your talent so you have the freedom to do challenging theatre projects. Like theatre auditions, you must understand that you are *being cast from the moment you enter the room*. Even more than for film or theatre, the people making the casting decisions have *no understanding whatsoever that actors can play many different kinds of characters*. Most cannot imagine an actor not being a specific *type*. They are really hoping you will offer them 'your character', so memorable, so original, so funny or so engaging that they will have *total certainty* you are the right actor to sell their product.

In creating commercials, for the most part, ad agencies imitate the successful commercials you are seeing each day. This gives you your first task. *Become obsessed with watching commercials*. You want to figure out which of these you would be *perfect* for. Try to identify actors that are *similar to you* in look, type and personality. This is because quite often the client will say, 'Get me an actor just like the one in the XYZ commercial.' I warned you. They lack imagination.

Next, try to jot down the scripts of some of those commercials so you can practise them. You want to feel totally at ease saying those words. And I want you to *commit to them* as fully as you would if this were Neil Simon or Alan Bennett or Anton Chekhov. The director says, 'You are a chilli pepper waiting to be wrapped into a fajita. It's your big moment.' The more deeply you can *feel the thrill* of being called to star in the fajita show, the more you will delight the owner of *Caliente Frozen Dinners*. As you experiment on your own with doing the commercials you are seeing, you will begin to develop a sense of the unique personality type you can offer. Does that mean it is the *only* type you will audition with? No. But you do want to know what your *strong suit* is – what first impression can you wow them with?

I'll give you a few hints. You can look for these ideas as you become an avid student of advertising. The humorous commercials often feature a clueless person – this can be a husband, wife or best friend – and another character who is wise, warm and loving. It is the clueless person who is the dramatic/comic centre – because they will be the one to 'learn' about the wonders of the product. *If you can perfect a charming stupidity you will earn money.*

Sometimes instead of having a script you will be asked to improvise a scene. There are many superbly gifted actors who find improvisation close to impossible. They have shared *nightmare memories of drama school humiliations*. Fortunately you can have a very successful career without this skill. It will mean turning down some commercial auditions, however, and the loss of that potential income.

Casting that requires improvisation can happen for several reasons. The script may still be unfinished and they are hoping you will provide ideas for them. *The commercial will be mostly your reactions to things with very little dialogue and they want to see how lively you will look and how interesting your reactions would be.*

Stay very open to what your fellow actors are doing – directors often shy away from an actor who wants to 'take over' or steal focus from others. Stay connected to your body and *try to keep the running commentary and direction from your Intellect at bay*. Always keep your reactions to children warm and loving! – these are not dramas about dysfunctional families!

Whatever the scenario, *if you are a dancing pickle or a super-cool computer geek*, **your job is to make it look like fun**. Don't get hung up on trying to write a clever script. They are looking for spontaneous reactions. They are looking for your daring and courage to go full out without editing and being 'careful'. Delight in each opportunity. Don't be surprised by how often they cast you.

Having a successful career and a successful life

I think of all the actors whose lives I have touched. I've watched with pride as they've been cast in films and on television series. I cheer as I see them onstage, glowing with spontaneity and emotions of such depth I can feel the entire audience moved to tears. I cheer just as heartily when they email me about the creative energy they are experiencing, their optimism and eagerness to engage fully in their lives.

I visualize you reading this book and hoping you, too, will have a life that is full of success and happiness, not just as an actor but in this grand drama we call 'our lives'. We are all 'works in progress', learning every day. We all struggle with our balancing act of the chattering Intellect, the wise conscious mind and the glorious Dungeon with all its mysterious secrets.

The heady pleasure you felt when you first acted and were not yet under the tyranny of your Intellect is yours now, all the time. Whether it's a staged reading, or a children's theatre production of *The Magic Peanut*, or a running part on a TV series or a leading role on Broadway – in the end, *it's always about sharing your broken heart, your rage, your hunger and your joy*.

The real adventure is when *your opened Dungeon* speaks to the feelings locked in the Dungeons of your audience. Their Dungeon doors crack open, light filters in and you have done your work as an actor. **You have transformed your pain, your struggles, your sadness and your joy into this wondrous thing we call 'art'.**

RESOURCES: PASSIONATE LIFELONG LEARNING

You are living in exciting times. At your fingertips is knowledge that either didn't exist or that would have taken ages to find just thirty years ago. Now Google can connect you to articles written in the fields of neuroscience and psychology, theatre history, costume design and beyond. There are also wonderful books that give you an in-depth picture of many things I've simply touched upon. **This is a list of my favourite books that have helped shape my thinking about acting. They have enriched, clarified and reinforced concepts and filled me with wonder.** I know you will find many more on your own – this is in no way an *exhaustive* bibliography. **I hope this list of books will *fuel your curiosity*.**

The brain

The Mind and the Brain, Jeffrey Schwartz, M.D. & Sharon Bagley (Harper Collins, 2003).
A fascinating look at the conscious and unconscious mind, with focus on OCD (obsessive-compulsive disorder) and innovative therapeutic approaches.

A User's Guide to the Brain, John J. Ratey, MD (Random House, 2002).
Written in conversational style with case histories to illustrate the interactions and workings of the brain. Ratey is a neuropsychiatrist

who teaches at Harvard Medical School. He describes the connections between the motor cortex and memory and emotion.

Spark, John J. Ratey, MD (Little, Brown and Company, 2008).
The most recent research in how exercise impacts memory and learning.

Mapping the Mind, Rita Carter (University of California Press, 2010).
Wonderful drawings, historical explanations, this book is filled with amazing information. Brain function can be overwhelmingly difficult. Carter is excellent at clarifying very complex systems.

The Brain that Changes Itself, Norman Doige, MD (Penguin Group, 2007).
A compilation of the research that demonstrates the plasticity of the brain throughout our lives. I find it incredibly inspiring.

Proust Was a Neuroscientist, Jonah Lehrer (Houghton Mifflin Harcourt, 2008).
Great fun. This little book explores examples of how famous people in the arts have intuited and demonstrated brain insights that have later been proved by neuroscience research.

Molecules of Emotion, Candace Pert, PhD (Scribner, 1999).
A researcher and pioneer in the mind-body world, Pert's landmark research in 1988 was the first to prove that there are 'opiate receptors' in the body. She believes that exploring emotions on a muscular level as we are doing in *acting with passion* strengthens the immune system.

Incognito, David Eagleman (Knopf Doubleday Publishing Group, 2012).
This book pulls together some of the latest ideas on the unconscious mind. Written with warmth and humour.

My Stroke of Insight, Jill Bolte Taylor, PhD (Penguin Group, 2009).
Filled with insights about right and left brain function discovered by this neuroanatomist as she observed herself having a stroke at the age of twenty-eight. Like Candace Pert, she suggests Bioenergetic exercises to open access to the right brain and the unconscious.

TED Talks (www.ted.com/talks) is the most extraordinary resource. If this is new to you, you are in for a treat. If you put in the topic of 'neuroscience' you will find a wide array of talks. Three of my most recent favourites are:

Jill Bolte Taylor (www.ted.com/talks/jill_bolte_taylor_s_powerful_stroke_of_insight)

Dr Charles Limb (www.ted.com/talks/charles_limb_your_brain_on_improv)

Bonnie Bassler (www.ted.com/talks/bonnie_bassler_on_how_bacteria_communicate)

Psychology

Bioenergetics, Alexander Lowen, MD (Penguin Group, 1994).
Lowen's classic book on Reich's mind-body approach, made more usable through Lowen's application. Lowen wrote many books on this subject, most of them giving more case studies and thus enriching his examples of the therapy. You will notice that his approach is grounded in Freudian psychology which may or may not make it as useful for you.

The Way to Vibrant Health, Alexander Lowen, MD (The Alexander Lowen Foundation Publishers, 2012).
Written with his wife, Leslie, and published in 2012, it is his most recent book. You can see that his thinking has evolved. He offers a series of exercises for general health, many of which are drawn from yoga.

Character Analysis, Wilhelm Reich (Farrar, Straus & Giroux, 1980).
Reich wrote many books. I believe he was a genius, but the books are long, complex and not easy to read. I think this is his most accessible. He was very much a product of his time – Germany in the late nineteenth century – and his close association with Freud. His obsession with orgasm reflects the level of sexual repression common at the time.

Family Kaleidoscope and **Family Healing**, Salvador Minuchin, MD (Harvard University Press, 1986).
Minuchin is my favourite psychotherapy guru. All of his books are inspiring, generous and optimistic. These two are a good place to start.

Mind as Healer, Mind as Slayer, Kenneth Pelletier (Random House Publishing Group, 1977).
A wonderful compilation of holistic healing.

Learned Optimism, Martin Seligman, MD (Knopf Doubleday Publishing Group, 2006).
One of the most straightforward, easy to follow books on cognitive therapy. It offers a practical guide if you are interested in exploring this form of therapy.

Uncommon Therapy, Jay Haley (W.W. Norton & Company, 1973).
A clear description of the innovative ideas of Milton Erickson – a genius whose work almost defies description. He seems to speak directly to his patients' unconscious minds.

Eye Movement Desensitization and Reprocessing, Francine Shapiro, PhD (Guilford Publications, 1995).
A truly remarkable new form of therapy, recreating REM (rapid eye-movement) sleep in an awake state. Especially effective for dealing with emotional trauma. I have witnessed remarkable healing through this form of therapy. It reinforces my belief that our unconscious mind wants us to be healthy and whole.

Strategic Family Therapy, Chloe Madanes (Wiley, 1991).
Partnering with Jay Haley, Dr Madanes offers a clear understanding of their creative approach to therapy. Haley is known for his 'paradoxical' instructions to patients. To me this is his way of tricking the Intellect to permit his patients to experience themselves in healthier ways.

Shakespeare

1599: A Year in the Life of William Shakespeare, James Shapiro (Harper Collins *Publishers*, 2005) and *Contested Will*, James Shapiro (Simon & Schuster, 2010).
If you love Shakespeare, you are in for a treat!

Shakespeare's Friends, Kate Emery Pogue (Praeger Publishers, 2006) and *Shakespeare's Education*, Kate Emery Pogue (Publish America, 2011).

Both Shapiro and Pogue have written many books, all valuable, I've listed the ones I feel are a 'must' if you love Shakespeare.

The Book Known as Q, Robert Giroux (Random House, 1983).

For years I found the sonnets very hard going. Many seemed impossible to understand. This book was like a magic door permitting entry into these complex works.

The Complete Works of William Shakespeare, a FREE app. Have it at your fingertips!

Your Passionate Lifelong Learning

Please contact me with your questions and insights. Whether you are curious, frustrated or triumphant, I am only a mouse click away. My website is: www.nikiflacks.com. If you are interested in teaching this approach to acting, I will be offering workshops at the Actors Centre in London shortly after this book is published.

MY IMMENSE GRATITUDE

How do I begin to thank the legions of friends, family, teachers, fellow actors, directors, costume designers, choreographers, from whom I have learned and to whom I owe so much? Their generosity and willingness to share their gifts inspires me every day of my life.

Writing this book I have tried to fold their wisdom and insights within its pages. So many others, however, have helped shepherd me through the challenges of transferring the ideas and experiences of many years from my head onto my computer hard drive. Without them, this book would never have been written.

First, my boundless gratitude to the Actors Centre in London's West End. It was Louise Coles and Michael John who first suggested to Bloomsbury Methuen Drama that I might have a book of interest to them. Even more important, for the past nineteen years, the Actors Centre has given me a 'home' where I have been free to explore the concepts in *acting with passion* with countless actors.

Will Timbers, beyond creating the illustrations, has been an invaluable collaborator. A sensitive, gifted actor, his ideas, questions and artistry are embedded throughout the book along with his beautiful drawings of brain and skeleton. My thanks to Dr Martin Lazar, a brilliant neurosurgeon and close friend, who offered me my first entry into the fascinating world of neuroscience. My wonderful 'theatre photographer', Joel Horovitz, who has learned to capture actors at just the perfect moment, has made it possible to include the faces of at least some of the actors who have shared my journey. My gratitude and hugs to them for their willingness to enhance the pages of this book.

Many thanks to Jenny Ridout at Bloomsbury Methuen Drama, Joshua Pawaar at RefineCatch Limited and Jon Ingoldby. They have offered guidance and encouragement throughout the publication process. My very special gratitude goes to John O'Donovan, my editor. I don't know if the book would ever have been completed without John's sense of humour, perceptions, insights and ability to criticize with so much kindness.Writing a book based on actor training that is intensely physical, intimate and active has been my primary challenge. How to put into book form the physical and emotional experience of my standing next to an actor, speaking directly to muscles through my touch? How to communicate that, although this approach brings access to great wells of tears and rage, my classes are filled with laughter and joy? Finding the path has been through the willingness of friends to read and reread various drafts, offering their reactions, questions and encouragement.

Kate Pogue, my cheerleader in chief and Scott Williams my 'long lost twin' were there from the beginning. My generous readers: Tom Jennings, Marianne McAndrew, Eilenn Rich, my daughter, Ashley Hecht, the wonderful playwright Mike Folie, my yoga teacher, Jodie Ruffy, and Trish Baillie – who teaches voice and Alexander – none of whom had ever studied with me and were therefore able to offer fresh takes on the material and helped me to clarify complicated and often bewildering concepts. Many of the actors I've taught have read assorted chapters, cheering and challenging me with their questions and comments. Thank you, thank you, all of you!

Writing a book and balancing an active life is quite a trip! My four children have been endlessly encouraging, keeping me laughing, always reminding me of how complex and incredibly rich the thorny territory of parenting and love can be. And my husband, Joel – a surgeon dealing with real life and death – has surrounded me with his unconditional love.

INDEX